PRIVATE
PAIN
It's about life,
not just sex …

PRIVATE
PAIN
It's about life,
not just sex ...

Understanding
Vaginismus & Dyspareunia

Ditza Katz, PT, Ph.D.
Ross Lynn Tabisel, CSW, Ph.D.

Katz-Tabi Publications

Women's Therapy Center
54-A Sunnyside Blvd., Plainview, NY 11803
(516) 576-1118
www.womentc.com

Book design by Charles McStravick
Cover design by Steven Guddat
Front cover photograph by Talli Rosner-Kozuch

The information provided in this book is meant
for educational purposes only and should not take the place
of medical and/or rehabilitative care. Clinicians and other
healthcare providers must undergo professional training and
develop necessary expertise prior to treating vaginismus.

ISBN 0-9700298-1-0
First Edition

Printed in Canada
at Kromar Printing Ltd., Winnipeg

"כל המקיים נפש אחת...כאילו קיים עולם מלא"

סנהדרין, דף ל"ז, עמוד א

❦ ❦ ❦

Whoever saves one life . . .
it is as if he had saved the entire world!

— Sanhedrin 37:1

Ross' Dedication

I dedicate this book to my children, Brett and Sloane.

Brett, you challenged me as a mother from the day you came into this world. From the time you were little, I always knew that you had a mind of your own, and once your heart took you to what you wanted to do you went with it. No mountain was too high for you to climb. You never looked backward. You believed in who you were and followed every dream you had. I have always admired your talents, perseverance and ability to accept difficult times. Watching you perform on-stage as a professional actor has brought me much happiness, but most of all, it gave me strength to know that I, too, could follow my dreams. I thank you for that and for always believing in me even during the "hard times." Although you get embarrassed when we talk about my being a "sex therapist," I know how proud you are of me by the strength of your hugs. This book is my gift to you!

My princess, Sloane—you have been a part of this book from the day it was first conceived. You have always been my inspiration. You have always cared so much for everyone, and always understood the time I needed to spend on my work. You never complained about the many meals we had to eat out, but rather took it in stride, saying, "We are a different family." You encouraged me to pursue my work even if it meant that you gave up on some activities with your friends. Your own determination allowed me to keep going no matter how tired I was. At your very young age, you have demonstrated wisdom that surpasses your age; and you have learned more at an early age than most children learn in a lifetime. You also have my deepest respect for holding on to your Blue Line, even if it is directed toward me! Perhaps someday, if you will want to, you will continue to carry the torch and keep our work alive. Sloane, you are an exceptional child, and I am lucky that you are my "little girl"—this book is a piece of my heart that I share with you.

To Barry, my "big brother" and good friend—thank you for sharing Ditza with me. If you were not who you are, this book might not have been written, nor our work accomplished.

Lastly, I want to thank my business partner and very special friend, Ditza—she knows the reasons why.

— *Ross*

Ditza's Dedication

To my husband, Barry, for your unconditional love and support. This book would not have happened if not for you.

To my mother:

A15975—This is her identification number. It is tattooed on the inside of her left forearm, in blue color. She knows this number very well. *I was never called by my real name,* she would explain. She can recite it clearly unlike her social security number, which does not stick. She heard her ID number called out for attendance twice daily. It designated her job. It became a vehicle for discrimination. And she has it, forever, as a reminder.

Shula (Zita) was seventeen years old, healthy and strong, when she was "chosen" to work in the death camp of Auschwitz. Her job was to dig water channels and to clean the gas chambers of ashes that only a few hours earlier were living people, just like her. Perhaps she even knew some of them, in a different form.

Her twin sisters had tattoos as well. They were designated to the experimental section of Auschwitz, undergoing medical and gynecological torture to explain the differences between the perfect (Aryan) race and the others. . . .

I must have first seen the tattoo when she cradled me in her arms, her newborn daughter, just five years after the liberation from Auschwitz. I never thought twice about it. I believed that every mother had a tattoo, and I would have one too when I became a mother. I learned the truth when I started school. Growing up in Israel, I was surrounded by survivors with emotional and physical tattoos. It was a way of life to see them, to hear their stories, to witness their pains, and to look, in vain, for answers and explanations for this horrific event of life.

And I clearly remember my mom's personal struggles. How, to this day, she must have a glass of water next to her bed. How she must have food available at all times. How she gets a knot in her stomach upon leaving on a trip, even a happy family vacation, a reminder of the transport trains to the camps. How she cannot approach the authorities with the simplest of requests, such as filing a document or asking the doctor to explain.

I vividly remember the day, in 1966, when, on her way to work, Mom ran into her Kapo—the woman designated by the Germans to be in charge of the barrack. Mom returned home as white as a ghost, shaken and emotionally paralyzed. Reliving the horror (and the harsh treatment by the Kapo) moved her across time, back to Auschwitz. It opened the wounds that were covered by the thin layer of avoidance. Even sleep was not an escape—Mom has not slept more than three to four hours a night since the camps.

Her whole family perished. All 150 of them, except for about ten who survived. Somehow, they wandered back to their home, dug out some hidden pictures and jewelry, saw their prosperous property occupied by hostile locals, and left again.

Attempting to go to Israel in 1947 as a passenger on Medina ("State"), the cargo ship that followed the famous ship Exodus, Mom was rerouted to a transit camp in Cyprus, with thousands of other survivors. Although they were not tortured there, conditions were similar to those in the death camps—cold, wet, hungry, confined.

The person who would be my father followed her from Europe to Cyprus and eventually to Israel in 1948. She did not really want to marry him but felt forced into it when he threatened to kill himself if she left. Mom could not face another death; she could not say *NO*.

So she continued to survive through the struggles of an unwanted and unhappy marriage, during hard economic times in the developing State of Israel, while constantly struggling with her own personal wounds.

Mom was, and still is, a wonderful mother. She showed me and my brother love and affection, she made us feel the best about ourselves, and she showed us how to go far and become successful—all while covering up her pain. Like all

Children of Survivors, we had to sort ourselves out, having been witness to pain and fear.

But as much as I have tried to come close to understanding these feelings, I am always miles away. My body does not have memories of fear . . . my stomach does not know hunger . . . my soul does not have incurable wounds . . . I can trust, confront, be hopeful, defend my space—I can even say *NO*.

Mom is so tired now. She divorced my father after twenty-four years of marriage and to this day she still feels ashamed. She was an outstanding professional and a successful businesswoman, but lost her fortune to events that were beyond her control. Her body is showing the wear and tear of a seventy-something fighter: Scars on her lungs from being beaten at Auschwitz, and circulatory problems from frostbite she suffered during the Death March on snowy terrain, forced by the Germans to flee from the Allies, killing anyone who could not keep up.

And her heart is tired too . . . tired of the memories; tired of fighting; tired of worrying about what will happen next. She misses her parents, her youth, and a lost love. Many of her friends are already dead, some are ill, and her social circle is constantly shrinking. She is planning her future, anticipating medical care, special services, and an old age home (she would not hear of her children taking care of her). What she is fighting to keep and protect so much is her dignity.

I want my mother to have the power, the voice, to make an impact. I want her to regain the rights she lost in Auschwitz. I hope this book proves that she is getting closer.

🌸🌸🌸

In just a few years the last living witness to the Holocaust will be gone.

WE MUST NEVER FORGET!

—— *Ditza*

Contents

Foreword

*K*nowledge is power. From the perspective of patient and physician, knowledge is the thorough understanding of all facets of a disease process, which leads to the ability to apply what is known to ameliorate or cure a pathologic process.

Stigmata attached to certain medical or sexual issues inhibit the ability of patients and clinician to achieve success and cure.

Vaginismus, the involuntary contraction of the pelvic floor muscles, is a condition beyond the control of the patient who suffers from it, in which knowledge and awareness portend to a more rapid diagnosis and treatment.

Silence, secondary to patient shame, is a tragic consequence of difficulty in diagnosis of this condition. This can lead patients to suffer silently for years without seeking help, or alternatively, spending years trying to obtain a cure for a disease that is often not easily recognized, not commonly taught or addressed, and not easily cured without expert, comprehensive treatment.

Women will commonly discuss with friends, and even strangers, a variety of gynecologic maladies. The media, in the form of magazines, radio, TV talk shows, and newspapers, commonly feature fibroids, pregnancy, abnormal pap smears, endometriosis, and infertility as topics of interest and active discussion.

Vaginismus, however, is a condition that is not addressed. Vaginismus patients often feel alone in their suffering because this condition is not commonly talked about. They are ashamed and often drift from physician to physician seeking out a diagnosis. These women may be unable to insert a tampon or undergo a vaginal exam of any kind. They may have been married for many years without ever having had intercourse because of the absolute inability to achieve penetration. They are scared, ashamed, and oftentimes develop significant problems in their personal, sexual, and marital relationships. They perceive themselves as "different," "damaged," and "incurable."

Emphasis on formal instruction in the etiology, diagnosis, and treatment of vaginismus is crucial in the training of new physicians in medical schools and residency programs alike. Prompt recognition, intervention, and assembly of a team of practitioners to comprehensively care for the vaginismus patient is paramount in achieving cure.

The team approach is the most important aspect of the care of the vaginismus patient. A brief office visit or a written prescription will not suffice for treatment. Rather, recognition of the problem by the physician with prompt referral of the patient for expert treatment by teams skilled in caring for this condition is crucial.

A combined approach of psychotherapy, pelvic floor physical therapy, and sex therapy offer the patient the most significant chance for resolution of vaginismus and cure. This team approach is best exemplified by the Women's Therapy Center, run by Dr. Ditza Katz and Dr. Ross Lynn Tabisel, where an atmosphere of understanding and a lack of stigmata, along with their intensive combined treatment approach, have led many of my own patients to a rapid cure.

I support and endorse the spectacular clinical expertise of these professionals, as well as their efforts to thoroughly educate the public and all medical practitioners about vaginismus. Their wealth of knowledge and experience come together to create a book that comprehensively covers it all.

— Wendy Fried, M.D., FACOG, FACS
Clinical Instructor,
New York University School of Medicine;
Attending Physician,
North Shore University Hospital,
Obstetrics and Gynecology

Acknowledgments

We thank our patients for allowing us to enter their innermost personal space while in their worst moments of distress and desperation and, subsequently, in happier times. We also thank their partners and/or family members who joined the painful journey toward life. All of you were our teachers as we were your guides, and this book could not have been created without your contribution.

Special thanks and appreciation to the following individuals who devoted time and energy to reading the manuscript and giving us their thoughtful input: Barry Saltsberg; Dr. Wendy Fried; Linda Sinowitz, ACSW; Allie; Ann; Beth; James; Mike; and Tara.

We are most grateful to:

Dr. Wendy Fried for believing in us and in our mission.

Dr. William Granzig for his support and guidance.

Sloane Tabisel for her research and for giving
the Blue Line an eternal life.

Whitney Sara Sinowitz for conducting her research
and for typing the result.

The doctors, rabbis, nurses, and other colleagues
who embraced our pioneering work.

And to the following patients and partners
who shared their intimate thoughts
and feelings for the book:
Allie, Ann, Beth, Dawn, Eric, Eve, Howard,
James, Jennifer, K.C., Katy, Kim, M.K., Mike, Paco,
S.B., S.M., Stefania, Tara, Tracy Morgan, Valerie,
and those who wished to stay anonymous.

INTRODUCTION

*V*aginismus and dyspareunia have been a cause of frustration to sufferers and clinicians alike. Women feel ashamed and inadequate and choose to suffer in silence rather than expose their inability to have vaginal penetrations. Healthcare professionals, on the other hand, can only find limited available resources for their search of how to manage and treat these conditions. The unfortunate outcome has been the continued, unresolved suffering.

Until now.

The pioneered work that is presented in this book is a culmination of many years of clinical practice that dared to explore, experiment, and think "outside of the box." Countless hours of data gathering were then dedicated to interpreting the enormous amount of clinical findings, leading to the authors' deep understanding and expert proficiency regarding vaginismus and dyspareunia.

This book is filled with real-life stories of both women who struggled with these conditions and partners who struggled along with them. These stories are unique in being the first to take such an intimate look at the impact and devastation of vaginismus and dyspareunia, as well as at the exhilaration of renewal and empowerment upon reaching a cure.

The reader, whether a sufferer or a professional, will be able to find detailed answers and comprehensive explanations as to the nature and treatment of these conditions, a much-needed source of information that is certain to fill the current void in the body of literature and research regarding these topics.

This book is a proof that professional education is dynamic and expandable, and that optimal patient care must believe in the body-mind connection.

The inspiring content of this book will, undoubtedly, serve to reassure women around the world that they are not the only one who suffers of this condition, and that— yes—there is a cure!

— William A. Granzig, Ph.D.
President, American Board of Sexology;
Dean and Professor, Department of Clinical Sexology,
Maimonides University, Miami Beach, Florida

CHAPTER ONE

Am I the Only One?

C an someone please help me? I am thirty years old, and I have suffered from vaginismus all my life.

The first time I saw a doctor, he told me I had "a head problem" and sent me to a harsh psychiatrist. This was over twelve years ago.

Since that time, I have gotten married, but I have not been able to enjoy a "normal" sexual relationship. While my husband, for the most part, has been loving and supportive, the dynamics of our marriage are changing and I fear that he is losing hope of us ever having a sexual relationship.

This is adding incredible stress to our lives . . .

Six years ago, feeling desperate and not finding any solutions, I underwent a painful operation that was supposed to enlarge the entrance to the vagina. The doctor told me that I had a very small entrance to my vagina (a small finger could barely enter) and the hymen was still intact. Recovery seemed to go on for three weeks and the pain was excruciating—worse than anything I had ever felt when trying to have intercourse.

Unfortunately, this operation did not solve the problem.

Two years later I underwent another operation in the hope that finally I would be ok. Alas, this operation did not work either and I don't know what to do.

Sadly, this desperate cry for help may be a familiar tune to many women who suffer from vaginismus—a condition that makes vaginal penetration either difficult (dyspareunia) or altogether impossible.

Every day, more women around the world discover that they have vaginismus, but the lack of answers and cure makes them feel hopeless and choiceless. Every day, at the Women's Therapy Center, women overcome this disorder and go on to leading healthy, normal life . . . In other words: *Yes, a cure is available!*

Common myths surround vaginismus and dyspareunia, such as it has to do with having a small vaginal opening, or with being "crazy;" with needing to relax, or with having a history of sexual abuse.

The truth is that vaginismus affects women both with small and with big vaginal openings; it is not related to any mental illness, and it has nothing to do with relaxing. And, contrary to common belief by many doctors and thera-pists, sexual abuse is just one of many reasons for this con-dition, and not at all the prime reason.

Another myth that is shared by healthcare profes-sionals and by the public is that vaginismus has to do with a structural deficiency of the vagina. The truth is that vaginismus is not a structural problem but rather a reac-tionary phenomenon whereby the vaginal canal is being "squeezed shut" when penetration is suggested, yet "opens up" when the threat of penetration is removed. Vaginismus is a panic attack in the vagina!

And another popular myth implies that vaginismus is caused by poor sexual skills—a statement that is the far-thest removed from the truth! Vaginismus is not about sexual performance or lack of sexual techniques, but rather about wanting to be "normal" yet being afraid of penetrations.

The misunderstood nature of vaginismus brings about feelings of shame and inadequacy, making the suffering woman feel like "I am the only one who suffers from this," "Even my doctor doesn't understand it," and "I must be a freak . . . weird . . . deformed . . . broken . . . hopeless." There is a great sense of "My body betrayed me" because of the inability to have simple penetrations such as inserting a tampon, applying medication, undergoing a gynecologic pelvic examination, or conceiving a child in a natural way. Some women feel that it's because "I don't love my partner enough," while others believe that "It's because my hymen cannot be penetrated."

The following is a quote from an e-mail we received from one of our former patients: . . . *[The process] wasn't easy, but easier than I thought it would be. One thing I wanted to share: Since I knew I had vaginismus, I had completely stopped thinking of the possibility that I could ever have kids; I stopped even being able to picture that day. And one of the things that is so wonderful now, is being able to feel that possibility again.*

The partner suffers as well, feeling helpless, frustrated, betrayed, and wondering about his or her own sexual competency. Being pinned between having to consider a breakup or resigned to having a limited sex life is a common dilemma.

Living in secrecy is the most common coping mechanism for dealing with the devastation of vaginismus and with the reluctance to admit and disclose the presence and details of the problem. With pain and sexual dysfunction being viewed as an abnormality, the lack of answers and solutions deepens the sense of helplessness and confusion even more.

The inability to consummate a marriage or a relationship is perceived as a personal failure, often forcing the couple to live a lie to their immediate family and closest friends by pretending to have a normal sex life. On the other hand, the single woman will choose to hide her anguish in embarrassment and in fear of being a social outcast. She will often avoid relationships, choose asexual partners, stay in a troubled relationship out of feeling sexually inadequate, wonder if she might be gay, or end a relationship when it becomes intimate.

The search for answers to vaginismus is typically long and frustrating. Physicians, therapists, and other health-care practitioners seem to be at a loss, often dismissing the case, or offering inappropriate measures for curing it, such as taking a drink, or smoking pot, or prescribing medications (Valium, Prozac, Xanax, etc.). The patient, in turn, feels misunderstood, neglected, isolated, and hopeless, and is forced to either resign to living with the "problem," or embark on an endless quest for finding a name for the problem, explanations, and a cure.

Nearly every woman who spoke with us tried to convince us that she is the *ONLY ONE* who suffers from this mysterious condition, a feeling shared by many male partners as well. In speaking with us, they were shocked to learn how common vaginismus is, not to mention their emotional relief upon personally speaking to and meeting other patients and former patients who now act as advocates.

This repeated scenario, coupled with a void in available up-to-date literature regarding vaginismus, prompted us to write this book, aimed at shedding light on the nature and impact of this condition, and on the treatment approach that has proven successful.

Our ultimate goal in writing this book is twofold: To bring vaginismus into the open and to raise global awareness so that sufferers will no longer feel alone and helpless, and to inspire clinicians to expand their professional horizons so that treatment for this condition will be readily available to anyone, anywhere in the world.

We hope this book will be an enlightening journey to partners, family members, and friends of women who suffer from vaginismus, as well as to physicians, especially those in women's health (gynecology, internal medicine, family practice, adolescent medicine, urology, urogynecology, etc.); medical residents; physical therapists, especially those who specialize in women's health; psychotherapists; clinical social workers; marriage counselors; sex therapists; sexologists; psychologists; nurses and midwives; physician assistants; members of the clergy; health educators; guidance counselors; teachers; lawyers (especially matrimonial); mikvah staff (women's quarters); health insurance representatives; media representatives—this condition needs publicity!

CHAPTER TWO

The Girl Without a Hole

The Girl Without a Hole
by Eve F.

I knew there was as problem when I was sixteen. I was at the park with some high school sophomores, male and female, and we were talking about the body and sex. I couldn't understand the concept of any-thing entering my body, and the thought of using tampons had also always unnerved me. Girls and women had emphatically told me numerous times that tampons were more comfortable and convenient than pads. I just couldn't bring myself to try. That night at the park I realized that I had no idea how my body worked. I did not even know where this opening was that could fit a tampon, finger, or even a penis. I figured that I should try to use a tampon to prepare myself for the other stuff, which still seemed to be in the distant future. As much as tampons had always freaked me out, pleasuring myself or allowing someone else to were thoughts I was not ready to even consider.

Later on that spring night two senior girls gave me a few tampons and, as a group, the other kids tried to explain to me how to use them. It was fun, in a way. Two of my guy friends and I even wrote a song about tampons and shot one into the fountain to watch it expand.

On a more serious note, my friend Katie and I decided that we would both try tampons during our next periods. I couldn't wait. Somehow I thought I'd feel more grown-up, more like a woman, once there had been something in my vagina. With the pressure of womanhood along with the fact that my friends all knew I was trying tampons, I was understandably nervous when my period arrived.

I marched alone into the bathroom and read the instructions on the box. It said nothing about how to find the hole that the tampon would be inserted into. The box simply instructed me to relax, place the tampon applicator into the vaginal opening, and gently glide it in. I was confused, but my friends would be waiting for the news so I had to figure out a way to make it work. I applied pressure with the tampon to the general region, but that part of my body felt completely solid; no area gave way to the pressure of the tampon. Overcome with fear of my body and devastated that something might be wrong with me, I let the tears stream down my face. After settling for a pad, I sat on the bathroom floor staring at the tampon box with disbelief that I was a failure at something that every woman can do.

When my friends found out about my lack of success, they made suggestions about using mirrors and trying to relax. They even brought me to the bookstore and we looked at pictures of exactly where the opening should be. Disconcertingly none of the pictures seemed to resemble what I could see in the mirror.

Katie's period came a week later, and I was relieved that the first time she tried a tampon, it didn't work either. However, she had found the opening. A few days later, she attempted the mission again and this time succeeded in inserting a tampon all the way. She tried to make me feel better by saying that she removed it after a few minutes due to discomfort, but that didn't matter to me. What mattered was that she knew she could do it.

For about a year I tried again every once in a while, using new tricks and relaxation techniques. I would not let anyone else try to help me or even be in the bathroom with me. Being an excessively private person, I would just have to deal with it on my own.

The situation became a joke among my friends. At some point their joking caused me to stop thinking about the seriousness of what I was going through. I could live without tampons and without masturbation. Also, since most of my friends were still virgins, I didn't feel pressured to have sex. My casual attitude toward the matter was also encouraged by the fact that no one *really believed that I didn't have a hole. I guess my friends figured it was just an attention ploy. It wasn't until I figured out just how known the story had become that the jokes stopped being so funny.*

One night I was at a concert in my town and an older guy who I had never seen before came up to me and asked, "Aren't you the girl without a hole?" Shocked and horrified, I turned and ran out into the parking lot. I stood in the dark trying to breathe. The night air spun around me. There were a few stragglers outside, but I had never felt so alone.

My empty feeling began to subside when in the spring of my junior year Shane, a guy who some of my friends were obsessed with, asked me out. I couldn't believe it. Of course I said yes. One night he asked me if I'd ever had sex. I instinctively returned to my joking mode and said that I couldn't because I didn't have a hole. I was surprised that he hadn't heard. He laughed thinking it was nonsense. "What am I going to do with you?" he asked playfully. "I don't know," I answered honestly, but with a deceivingly lighthearted smirk.

After a few months of dating, Shane and I did attempt intercourse. We had been drinking a little and the situation was not something we had planned. He was not a virgin. Supposedly he was quite experienced, so naturally I thought that he'd be able to simply find my hole and make it work. No such luck. We poked around together and I just became upset. It was use-less and I felt like a failure once again. This was the end of Shane and me, but more importantly, it was the proof I needed to make everyone understand that I really didn't have a hole. I recently found out that

Shane and his friends made fun of my lack of a hole when I wasn't around. They had actually challenged each other to try to sleep with me to see who could be the first to find it. I was not aware of this as it was happening, but I am not sure it would have mattered.

I only cared about being like other people my age. I was dumbfounded as to why my body didn't work. By this time I was so fed up that I asked my mother to make a gynecological appointment for me. Two days before my eighteenth birthday, I went to see a doctor. I couldn't explain myself without a burning feeling in my eyes and pools of water forming above my cheeks. Unfortunately, the doctor was not nearly as moved by my story as I was. It seemed as though she didn't believe me any more than Shane had when I had first broken the news to him.

In the examination room the gynecologist said that she didn't need to use the speculum on me and that she'd start with a Q-tip. I was shocked that she'd even mentioned the word speculum. The thought of anything at all inside me seemed impossible. I certainly hadn't been considering that she might attempt to fit a speculum into my nonexistent opening.

The doctor neared the area with a Q-tip, but it didn't make it past the surface. I was crying violently. It really did hurt. She tried several times and then told me to get dressed. I was so disappointed in myself. I had thought that everything would be better after my visit. Once again, my friends were waiting to hear the news. Professional confirmation of my fear that I didn't have a hole was not the news I'd had in mind. When the doctor returned to the room to talk to me, she said that

one of her friends had been like me and she had "got-
ten over it." She said that psychotherapy might help
and gave me the number of someone local, but I didn't
think there was any point in seeking therapy for a
problem that really did not exist. I was devastated
and hopeless. I was not any better, and I was not even
headed in the direction of overcoming my problem.
I thought I was destined to be "holeless" forever.

A month or two later my friend Scott was reading
an informational sex book at my house with another
friend. The thought of sex made me too sad to pay
attention to them, so I sat alone watching television.
Suddenly Scott jumped up and rushed the book over to
me. He pointed to a bold print word and exclaimed,
"This is it! This is YOU! This is what you have!"
Vaginismus, it read. There was only a tiny blurb, but
it did describe me. This was what I had!

That night I searched the Internet and printed out
a folder's worth of information. The steady stream
pouring from my eyes blurred my view of the screen, but
I could see enough to experience the relief of knowing
that my problem had a name and I was not alone.

One day, shortly after that wonderful night,
I tucked my folder under my arm and returned to the
office of the same gynecologist I had seen a month
earlier. "I know what I have," I said bravely, pointing
to the label.

"Yeah, I know," she said, "I have it written down."
She showed me her notes. Vaginismus was scribbled
on the page. I was speechless. When I had composed
myself a little I asked through tears, "Why didn't
you tell me?"

She answered that she thought it would have been pointless because I had never heard of vaginismus. I told her just how much better I had felt when I had discovered it was a real disorder with a name, something that other people had too. She shrugged her shoulders and reminded me that she had told me about her friend who had it. Obviously, though, she hadn't made it clear that what her friend had "gotten over" was a disorder. I left her office feeling angry and let down. The doctor did schedule a meeting with a psychotherapist for me, though.

I started seeing Terry, the psychotherapist, in February and stayed with her until August, right before I left for my first semester in college. Terry knew nothing about vaginismus or how to cure it. In fact, during my second visit, she had to pull out her medical dictionary and look it up. She spoke to me of possibly going to treatment with dilators. As far as I could tell, I would never be ready for that as long as I was completely impenetrable.

Looking back, I think her sessions may have hurt me further. Terry was a religious woman and she tried convincing me that wanting to have sex at this point in my life was wrong. Before I started therapy, I hadn't thought that way. My parents had always seemed to have a more open view of sex. Even before I had started my period, my mother had "the sex talk" with me. She told me that I was to let her know as soon as I wanted to "be intimate" with someone so that we could take the appropriate precautions.

Terry wasn't going to be able to change the beliefs I had grown up with, but she did set me off course for *a while. She carried her belief to the extreme and re-iterated often that I should concentrate on finding someone who didn't want to have sex. She thought that if I met the right person, I'd magically be cured. I did not think this was true, but I could not make her understand. Her little explanation didn't cover the tampon problem, but arguing became tiresome, and I guess I kind of gave in and started living according to Terry's words. I began hanging out with a new set of friends, one quiet boy in particular, who hadn't wanted to have sex with his last girlfriend, my close friend Jessica. Nothing really happened between him and me, because although I valued him as a person, I realized that the main reason I had developed feelings for him was that he didn't want to have sex. His atti-tude toward sex potentially could change at any time.*

Once I realized that I'd been doing this and decided, undoubtedly, that I did not want to live according to Terry's relationship advice, my goal for my therapy appointments shifted. For the last three months we only talked about college and how to cope with meeting new people. Terry would not let me say that I was different from the people I'd meet.

When I arrived at college, however, I discovered that I actually was different. Everyone talked about sex. The few students I met who didn't have sex had made a conscious decision to wait for various admirable reasons. In contrast, I felt embarrassed and hopeless. At least these people knew they'd be able to have sex someday, if they wanted to. I felt more out of place than ever.

Despite my weak self-image, I started seeing a guy named Erik in early October. He closely fit the image

I'd envisioned of the perfect college boy, so I was afraid of messing things up. I feared my disorder would be the end of any sort of relationship with him.

With refreshed determination, I dove into the Internet again. This time I discovered The Women's Therapy Center, a place that actually specialized in vaginismus! I nervously made a call to the center, expecting to wait for months before being fit into the schedule, but they had an opening in less than a week. I was also lucky that my school schedule worked out so that I didn't have Friday classes and therefore had that day open every week for appointments. The setback was that the place was located almost four hours away from my school and about two-and-a-half hours away from my house in Connecticut. My family had to make sacrifices to overcome the distance. My parents, who had been supportive all along, agreed to help me with transportation since I didn't have a car. On Thursday nights my father would pick me up and drive me to our house, which is two-and-a-half hours away from school. On Friday mornings I would drive to Long Island for two-hour appointments and then drive back home. In the evening one of my parents would drive me back to school. This arrangement was to take a larger toll on my energy and therefore on my academic work and social life than I had anticipated. But at my first appointment I knew it was the right decision. For the first time, I felt real hope that I had a chance of getting better.

Once involved in appointments, the problem was that trust is a big issue with me. I don't trust people in everyday life and two professionals, the gynecologist *and the psychotherapist, had both let me down. Being able to trust Ditza and Ross was going take a miracle.*

Privacy was another big issue. The thought of other people looking at and touching my body anywhere was more difficult for me than anything I'd ever been through. Because it was that part of my body in particular, which had already been checked out without success, made the situation seem impossible. I hated the idea of someone getting to know my private parts through what seemed like inspection, week after week.

After several sessions, Ditza and Ross finally said that there was nothing more they could do unless I made the leap from the "safe" counseling room with three comfortable chairs to the "scary" treatment room with medical furniture and supplies. They explained that their method was to combine the physical work with the mental/emotional work. Besides, talking with my last psychotherapist had not improved my disorder, and I hadn't figured out my body on my own. Realizing all of this, however, did not mean that I was passively going to waltz up to the table and jump under the pink paper blanket. I made one last attempt at preventing the humiliation of being looked at and touched. I asked Ditza and Ross to show me pictures in books and to explain in the clearest details possible how to find my opening on my own. Determined, I ventured alone into the bathroom, clutching a mirror and a book with diagrams for one last attempt. When again I was unsuccessful, I felt as though I had to hand the control over to them. Just like the gynecologist had a year earlier, she took a Q-tip and touched the opening with it. The fear was so strong that the next time I went to the office I claimed that I needed a break from the "scary" room. The other room was much more comfortable; in it, I could sit upright, fully clothed, confident that nothing in sight might try to find its way to my opening. Ditza and Ross agreed to give me the day off from the" scary" room, but again said that I needed that room to get better. They repeated something to me that they had been saying for a few weeks, that I was "sabotaging my recovery." I didn't understand what that meant and I certainly didn't think it was true. They seriously told me to consider not coming back.

When I did return the next week, I told Ditza and Ross that I needed to stay because I had no other options. I had a new solution, though, that I thought they could help me with. I wanted to be put to sleep and be examined so that I knew I at least had the parts. I understood that I would still need to visit the therapy center and work on slowly getting better, but it would be easier to work toward something that was actually there.

Obviously, they were strongly against my plan. I had almost been too afraid to bring it up, because I had anticipated their reaction, but hearing their reason for being against it was important to me. As with most of our conversations in the beginning, Ditza and Ross were unable to make me understand completely. We disagreed for a while, and then I changed the subject and again asked how I was sabotaging my recovery. I expected this to create more problems, but I still thought I should attempt once more to understand, especially since there was a chance that I might not be returning to the Women's Therapy Center.

Surprisingly they did answer the question differently this time. They gave me specific anonymous examples of how quickly other patients had braved the "scary" room and how their successes were achieved. This was a definite breakthrough and turning point for me. Knowing that Ditza and Ross had helped others had never had a great impact on me before until I realized how important it had been for the others to trust.

The next visit was the last one before my long winter break from college. We did the "tour of my parts," which consisted of Ditza pointing to and naming the parts of my vaginal area while I watched in the mirror. I think it was the most difficult thing I've ever had to do. Then using the Q-tip as a pointer, she showed me the opening. That was all I would allow for the day. I was pretty shaken up, but now I knew I had an opening.

That same weekend, back at school, I met Josh at a party. Erik and I had stopped seeing each other without even discussing it and now it was about time for me to move on.

One night Josh and I were in my bedroom making out and he said, "Hold on". He rummaged through his backpack and pulled out a condom. Oh no! Now I'd have to tell him and ruin everything. It was my turn to say, "Hold on." I told him I had something to tell him, but no more words came out. He looked at me with concern and that helped. After about ten minutes of him comforting me, I was able to tell him about my disorder. He hugged me and told me that it was okay. I was shocked because the last two times I had told someone I was headed into a relationship with about my disorder, it had scared them away.

That doesn't mean that Josh and I were unaffected by my vaginismus. The problem was that I did want to have intercourse with him. I felt uneasy around him sometimes when I couldn't keep from dwelling on my insufficiency. There was a positive side, though: My disorder was improving rapidly because now I was working on getting better for him, just as much as for me.

I moved right along, each session with something new. First Ditza's gloved finger, then a tampon, and then the various-sized spacers [dilators of different types, some being anatomically correct].

I was feeling accomplished, but not satisfied. I wondered what would happen in a real situation with a guy. I was more comfortable letting guys see and touch my body than I was with doctors, but that didn't mean that intimate situations were easy for me. Erik and Josh had both discovered that I was unbelievably ticklish. I squirmed when they touched any part of my body and moved quickly away when they neared the lower region. But my body was working against my thoughts and emotions because I liked making out and I wanted to be able to go further.

During spring break I was visiting Josh and I told him how well I was doing. He said he was proud of me and I knew it was genuine. That night he was able to finger me, inserting his finger completely. I was enthralled that I had been able to do this much with a guy. We talked about doing more. Josh felt a great deal of pressure because he really only wanted to go further if I'd enjoy it. I tried to explain to him that I would be happier than ever before if I could just prove to myself that I could have intercourse. I then added that women usually don't have orgasms through intercourse; that clitoral stimulation was required. He didn't want to believe me. We attempted nothing more that weekend. Soon after, our long-distance relationship faded out and I actually never saw him again.

A few weeks later Ditza and Ross held a meeting for a group of their patients with vaginismus. I had attended one such meeting before, but this time I was offered to be a speaker because of my progress. At nineteen years old I was their youngest speaker and I didn't know how the older women would react to my story. Amazingly, I had the room crying and laughing at my failures and successes. That meeting marked one of the most satisfying moments of my life to date.

I went back to college in the fall with more confidence, but I was still feeling like a pathetic nineteen-year-old virgin. I spent the first four days of school feeling sorry for myself, but then I started having fun. I wasn't seeing Ditza and Ross as often, so I was able to rest on Fridays and catch up on work. I had more energy to go out on the weekends and meet new people. All I wanted was "to have sex for real" and know that it was intercourse as it happened. I felt hopeless, though, because there seemed to be a serious guy drought at school that semester. But one night I was on my way to a party with some friends and Erik was walking toward us from the opposite direction. I hadn't really spoken to him in almost a year, but for some reason he decided that this was a good time to start a conversation with me. We talked for a few minutes and I realized that I probably had a chance with him again. At this point he no longer seemed like the unattainable marvel that I'd thought him to be during my first semester of college.

For the next few weeks he was talking to me more and more and I couldn't put the thought of having sex with him out of my head. I ran it by Erica, the friend who had been seeing him, and she seemed to think it was a great idea. I was nervous about presenting the idea to my other friends, but by the weekend of the Halloween Dance I finally got up the nerve to tell them. Luckily they were supportive and wanted to help. We were dressed as Greek goddesses, me being Artemis, the goddess of the moon, the hunt, and virginity!

The dance was held in my dorm hall. At one point during the night, I had to run upstairs to my room to retrieve something, and on the way back down I ran into Erik, who was standing on the stairwell below me. He smiled up at me and complimented my costume. I smiled back encouragingly. From that point on, I knew I could do it. Much later that night we ended up in his room on his bed. He noted that I was no longer ticklish. It was true. I hadn't realized that. I felt very comfortable, so I asked him if he had a condom. He was surprised. The year before he had known that I wouldn't sleep with him, but he didn't know why. I told him that so much had happened in the past year. I think he wanted to know more, but he didn't push me. We were able to have intercourse without any problem.

I do feel better about relationships and about myself. I mean, I can wear tampons, can have a thorough gynecological exam, and can have intercourse. Also, because of my therapy, I am quite knowledgeable about sex. Even my most experienced friends come to me with questions, which was never even a glisten of a dream in my mind. As I approach my twentieth birthday, my confidence is ten times as high as it was a year ago.

Best of all, I am no longer known as "the girl without a hole"!

CHAPTER THREE

Internet Inquiries

The Internet has been a source of instant access to information in the search for understanding vaginismus, whether in medical literature or in publications for the general public. Men and women now have the opportunity to read and learn about the condition, to explore treatment options, and to find reassurance that they are not "the only one who has this. . . ."

From the first day we started posting information about vaginismus on our Website, we began to receive numerous daily inquiries, written by men and women from around the globe, all asking for information about this complex and mysterious condition.

As we are writing this book, our Website receives over two thousand inquiries monthly, all sending a loud and clear message: *Help! Nobody seems to know what to do!*

We decided to include the following inquiries because they represent a cross section of this condition, describing the devastation vaginismus has on the woman, on her life, on her partner, and on their relationship:

- I am suffering from vaginismus and have never had an orgasm. I have undergone a wide range of therapies and am at present consulting with a sex therapist. So far no success. I would like to know if you have any contacts in New Zealand and also whether you would recommend the use of antidepressants or short-acting tranquilizers. I am twenty-nine and have been in my present relationship for eight years. I love my partner and I have no recollection of a reason for my sexual dysfunction. I have had a pelvic exam under general anesthesia and this proved normal.

- I am writing to you because I need desperate help. I suffer from vaginismus. I am thirty years old and have never had intercourse. I have been to many psychologists and no one can help the problem. I have a horrible time with gynecologists. I have been married to my husband for several years and feel that my marriage is going in the tubes due to *my* problem. Any suggestions on what I can do to convince myself that intercourse is okay?

I have horrible panic attacks when it comes to the thought of having intercourse. My greatest fear is the pain it's going to bring. Please respond as soon as you possibly can. Scared and Anxious.

🐦 My wife and I have been married for just over four years. To date we have been unable to completely enjoy sex because penetration is painful to her. I learned that her sister and other women in her family had given her the impression that initial intercourse is *always* painful . . . Her gynecologist examined her and didn't find anything wrong . . . She began to get paranoid and tried to hide the pain from me. It was eating me up, because I figured that she wasn't physically attracted to me and that it was lack of lubrication that was the culprit. Well we've tried the *Lubrication Avenue*—gallons of it. Still no good . . . She began to make excuses and start fights whenever I would initiate intimacy (she never initiated). We've tried some relaxation exercises but she is unable to voluntarily relax those muscles. Can you help?

🐦 I am twenty-eight years old and I just realized that I am not crazy! After reading your Website, I think I may suffer from vaginismus. I live in Alabama—far away from your New York clinic. Can you refer me to someone in my area that can help me? Over the years, I have given up dating, social events, and any dreams of marriage/family. I am at the end of my rope. Please, please, please respond.

🐛 I am eighteen years old and the first time I had sex, I experienced pain and frustration like I never have before! My boyfriend could not penetrate me without unbearable pain, and I bled A LOT. We tried to use lubrication, doses and doses of it, yet that didn't seem to help. Recently, we tried again, but it was the same. I am very frustrated, and am beginning to worry if I could ever have sex again! What I can't understand is how little there is on the subject.

🐛 I am nineteen years old. I have been sexually active for three years, and have always found sex to be a painful experience. My doctor couldn't find any cause except sensitive skin, and my gynecologist said that lots of women suffer pain but "get over it." Can you offer me any suggestions about the next step to take in seeking your advice?

🐛 I have been married for two months now and feel exactly like some of the women on your Website. Intercourse just doesn't seem to work. Doctors have told me to try sticking a finger up—but it's really painful, so I stopped. Tampons get stuck about halfway and will go no further. It's all very frustrating. I live in Europe. Is there anyone here whom you can recommend for us to speak with?

❧ I am twenty-six years old, and I suffer from vaginismus. I have been married for just over a year and have been unable to have intercourse with my husband. I have a hard time talking to anyone about this—my husband is the only one that knows. It is a secret I carry with me. My friends all joke about intimacy and a lot of them are pregnant. I just think to myself that I will never be able to have children. There is nothing more I want right now than to cure this condition. It is sinking me into depression! It is on my mind day and night as it is on my husband's as well. I don't know how to start the process to recovery or where to turn. I really need help! I feel so embarrassed! Can you recommend anywhere for me to go? How quickly can something like this be cured? I cry so much about this and I really need to do something before it wrecks my marriage and me as well.

❧ I have tried everything to find a doctor. Most people ask me what vaginismus is and have never even heard of it. So now I'm beginning to think I'm crazy again and crying all the time. I can't believe that as many women as they say are affected by this that there is not more help for them. Practically none at all. I don't know what we're supposed to do but continue on as I have for years and try to force myself to have sex and go to the doctor. I've been trying to get drunk and have sex so maybe I can go to the doctor and get examined. I don't know what else to do. Why doesn't anyone know about this condition?

☞ I just read the story on your Website regarding the newlywed couple and felt relieved to finally hear that someone else out there has experienced what I am currently experiencing. My husband and I have been married for several years and only recently I finally got up the nerve to tell my gynecologist what was going on. She told me she has heard of this only one or two other times and couldn't give me much direction as far as who to see or what to do. Her suggestion was to try and relax and use a lot of K-Y. I need help, we need help! My husband has been very patient, however it is wearing on our marriage. I want desperately to have children. I am still a virgin! I also read that usually this happens to people without a high level of education because they don't take steps to research and communicate. This made me feel even worse as both of us are professionals . . . I understand that there is no quick fix. We will do whatever is necessary. I understand that you must receive many e-mails, however I would appreciate if you could respond as soon as possible.

☞ I live in Alaska, am thirty-four years old and I have been married for just about five years. Unfortunately, to date, I have been unable to ever have sexual intercourse with my husband,

and we are seriously thinking about having children within the next two to three years. I had a hymenectomy three years ago hoping that it would finally resolve my problem (of which I have been aware for at least the last decade), but it did not. In addition, my husband and I have been in counseling (sex therapy and marital counseling), I have tried dilators, lighting candles to create a romantic atmosphere, individual sex therapy, counseling, and been seen by several OBGYNs over the last ten years. I am *so* frustrated and at my wit end in dealing with this. My husband is and has been wonderful and patient, but the situation is not fair to him or me. Can you please help me? Any suggestions or referrals you can offer would be *very much appreciated.*

🍃 I'm writing on behalf of my wife and myself. I am married for several years to the best woman I could ever hope to find, but have never been able to have intercourse. The times we have tried, and they have become fewer over the years, penetration has been impossible. She complains of severe vaginal pain and I feel very badly over the situation and am bothered by the torment that she goes through each time we have tried. She has had two gynecological examinations and has been told, "Everything is okay." We have given up . . . She would "kill me" if she knew I was taking this to someone else. Is there anything you can do to assist or recommend to us regarding this problem?

🐞 I am a healthy twenty-seven years old woman who has been married for six years to the most wonderful man in the world. We were both virgins when we married and looked forward to our wedding night and the nights to come. But like your testimonials on vaginismus, it wasn't all we had dreamed it to be. After two years of marriage, we finally decided to try and get some help. My doctor suggested either getting pregnant or having surgery . . . I had the surgery hoping for a cure, but it was a lot of money down the drain with still a nonsexual relationship. It has been four years since that and we are still looking for answers. We appreciate any response and *thank you* for the diagnosis we have been looking for in the past six years.

🐞 I am twenty-three years old and have yet to be able to have a gynecological exam. I have been trying for five years with the same midwife who has been giving me birth control pills to keep my periods regular. I just recently got married and this is destroying my life. Sex is an issue too because I just don't feel like having it. The lack of this exam is tearing my self-esteem down. It has been for years. All of these different doctors keep telling me, "Don't worry, you're just not ready yet" or "It will happen when you are ready."

This is not good enough for me. I want to have answers, and now! I found your Website while searching the Internet and there was a story about a girl that was exactly like me! I couldn't believe it. No one, except my mom, understands how difficult this whole thing is for me. Please send me back an e-mail , I am desperate!

🍒 I have had this condition for far too long and even had my marriage break up because of it. I am ready to do whatever it takes to get better but I'm not sure what that is. I had laser surgery several years ago but it didn't help.

🍒 I am twenty-three years old and have been married for two years; sex is painful for me. It has always been painful and my husband doesn't know why. I've gone to a doctor many times to see what was wrong. I even changed birth control prescriptions because of the symptoms. I have burning, dryness, and just overall pain. Every time I think about having sex, it's like "Will it hurt?" I know it's not normal to be this way, but no doctor has given me any answers. They say there's nothing medically wrong with me . . . My husband thinks it's all psychological, but would that alone cause the pain?

🍒 My girlfriend and I have been together for around three years. She decided around a month ago that she would lose her virginity to me, and to her absolute horror found that she was unable to be penetrated. She said that she's just too tight and was really upset. Anyway, last week we tried again and once again she could not be penetrated. She was so upset by it she said she just had to go. I didn't know what at all to do, so I turned to the Internet for answers. We are too poor for therapy, and I doubt anyone here, in Brazil, would know where to start anyway. I really don't know what to do. Is there anything you could advise us to do at home? Please help us, we are really desperate.

I am a twenty-four years old married female who is suffering from vaginismus. I want to get help but I don't know even the first thing to do. I am so embarrassed. I went to an OBGYN and she told me just to get drunk and it would be okay. Well that did not work at all. I am so depressed about this and I want to beat this battle.

I have just completed reading your Website regarding painful sex. My twenty-year-old daughter has just told me of her problem in this regard, and I am at my wit's end with anguish trying to help her. She has visited our family doctor (before she told me of the condition) and the doctor really hasn't said or done anything. She (the doctor) thinks the condition will improve over time . . . My daughter suffers from frequent bladder infections and I also recall her telling me that she just couldn't use a tampon when she was in high school. Can you tell me if there are any specialists in Australia, where we live? Thank you for your wonderful Website information. Looking forward to hearing back from you.

I have been married for eight months and clamp up upon penetration. I haven't tried to force it in because I am afraid. I am deathly afraid of the gynecologist. I have been to one sex therapist that dismissed vaginismus as a possibility because she says it is only for rape or abused victims. So I switched therapists and now this therapist hasn't ruled it out but rather thinks I may have anxiety disorder. Just because I answered yes to five of her questions: Do you ever have sweaty palms, feel panicked, have any sleeplessness or hard-to-fall-asleep nights, afraid of dying, etc. Well, now her attention is on anxiety disorder! I just want someone to help me, not label me.

I am writing to you regarding a sexual problem that my girlfriend has. She's Asian and too shy to write for herself so she told me to do it. From a young age she's been told that sex is very bad, especially before marriage; that having a boyfriend is bad, and that you've got to have a husband straight away. She's worried to death about the first time we'll have sex once we get married, especially because she heard from other girls that it's very painful . . . So, we want to know, how to make that first time as painless as possible physically and, more importantly emotionally. Please help.

🐣 I am seventeen years old and live in the U.K. I was so relieved when I found your site to hear that what I suffer from was not unique to me and that I am not a freak. I first started thinking that there was something up with me when I was twelve years old and tried to use my first tampon. It would not go in. I thought that I must be built small, but after three years of trying, I did it, yet I still now find it painful to insert. I have recently split up with my boyfriend because foreplay alone scared me already. I do not know what to do—I dread going through life without a partner because I can't have sex. I know that this must sound really silly but I need some help and do not know where to go. I do not want to go to my GP [General Practitioner] as I have heard that most doctors are pretty oblivious to the disorder, and I am afraid that he will just send me away. All I ask is that you please reply and help me. It is so hard as none of my friends or family knows about this—I just need someone to talk to me and explain exactly what is wrong. Your site has already provided me with some relief. At least I know now that it is not only me, but also I need to find a way to stop it from happening. I hope to hear from you soon.

❦ My husband and I were both virgins on our wedding night. I had heard that there might be a little discomfort the "first time" and I wanted to make sure everything would be okay . . . So after snuggling for a while and using the K-Y Jelly we had packed along, he tried to slide his penis inside me for the first time. At first I thought he must have "missed the mark" because it felt like there was no way that space was designed for an object that size! If he tried to go in further, it would hurt. We stopped and began to pore over sex books we had brought to figure out what we were doing wrong. I took hot baths hoping it would relax me, but try as we might, we could not have sexual intercourse. We returned from our honeymoon with our marriage "un-consummated." The day after I called and scheduled an appointment with the doctor. When the receptionist taking appointments asked why I wanted to see the doctor, I told her it was for painful intercourse. I could hear her and the other girls in the office start to giggle about that. "You think that is *funny*?" I demanded angrily. She quickly hushed the other girls up and got me an appointment right away. I remember how my cheeks burned with anger by my pain being treated like a joke. When I described my experience to the doctor, he said casually, "Well, you're probably just having a little vaginismus." I had never heard that term before. He said that it was

an involuntary tightening of the vaginal muscles. He suggested that I look into psychotherapy to overcome any negative feelings and anx-
ieties I might have about sex. I told him that I
didn't have any particular hang-ups about sex
and while not obsessed with it, was looking forward to it, not dreading it. I was confused and
started to hear myself think, "What is wrong
with me?" My husband and I decided to just
relax and perhaps the problem would go away.
It didn't. I saw another gynecologist who wrote
me a prescription for painkillers and a cream to
completely numb myself before we planned to
have sex. It actually was better than nothing
and we had some "success" with that method,
but it numbed my husband's penis too and
killed any spontaneity, and I began to wonder
what was the point of having intercourse at all
if we couldn't feel anything. That was several
years ago and it was the last time I saw anyone
about this problem. I had pretty much given up
on this and was grateful that my husband was
basically content with nonpenetrative sex. Still,
I always feel a mixture of irritation, confusion,
and sadness that I am unable to enjoy the feeling of my husband inside me as millions of
women apparently can.

CHAPTER FOUR

What Is Vaginismus?

O ur goal for writing this book was to provide the most comprehensive and detailed explanation of vaginismus, a complicated medical condition and an intricate neurophysiological phenomenon.

It would have been quite simple for us to use medical terminology and scientific language, but we would have disappointed the real audience for this book: the women who suffer from vaginismus and their partners, family members, and friends. Instead, we chose to write using simple language that may be easily understood by all readers regardless of their educational background.

So, what is vaginismus? Let us divide the explanation into three components:

🐚 The basic definition

🐚 The medical explanation

🐚 The functional outcome

The Basic Definition

Many women, and certainly most of those who suffer from vaginismus, are not aware of the anatomy of their genitals, usually perceiving the area as a "big blob of skin." We encourage all female adolescents and women to familiarize themselves with their bodies in general, and their genitals in particular, through reading (see suggested reading list in the last chapter) and through body exploration.

To better understand vaginismus, the following are a picture and a short explanation of the components that make up the female genitalia:

🐚 **Pubic hair:** Varies in length, color, and volume. Some women trim it short, some shave it, some wax it off, but most women just leave it alone. Either way is fine, as long as it is the woman's own choice, and not done reluctantly, or just to please her partner.

🐚 **Outer lips (or Labia Majora):** The external thick folds of skin, one on each side of the midline, on which the pubic hair grows.

🌸 **Inner lips (or Labia Minora):** Thin internal skin folds, one on each side of the midline, that are visible once the outer lips are pulled open. The size of the inner lips may vary among women. In some women they may protrude between the outer lips; in others they will be contained within them; they may be equal in length, longer on one side than the other, or nearly "missing" altogether; their color may also vary, etc.

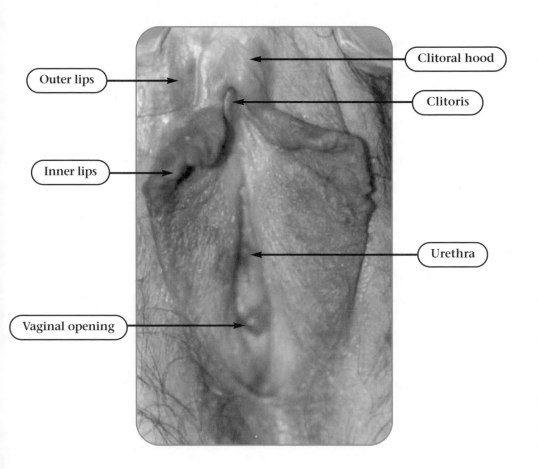

Clitoral hood

Outer lips

Clitoris

Inner lips

Urethra

Vaginal opening

🐾 **Clitoris:** The female's sexual stimulation zone. Its tip, known as the clitoral glans, is located at the top of the inner lips under a skin fold—clitoral hood—that can be pulled up to uncover it. The tip of the clitoris may be hidden under the hood, or quite visible by protruding from under the hood. Either way is normal. When touched, the clitoral tip feels like a small pebble. During sexual arousal, it will swell and become hardened— female erection. The body of the clitoris forms two "legs," each situated along the outer lips from the inside and is not, therefore, visible.

🐾 **Urethra:** The urine outlet—is the opening to the tube that leads to the bladder. The urethra is located within the inner lips and is surrounded by fatty tissue that serves as a protective cushion, giving it the appearance of a "blob" of flesh, as if surrounded by bubble wrap.

🐾 **Vaginal opening (or Introitus):** Located within the inner lips at the very bottom of the genital oval, just below the urethra. The vaginal canal itself continues into the pelvis and ends at the cervix, which is a "donut-like" structure, with a small opening in the center, that serves as the entrance to the uterus (womb). Contrary to some women's worry, the penis cannot and will not enter the cervix during intercourse.

❦ **Vulva:** A general term for the external parts of the female genitals—the outer and inner lips, the clitoris, the urethra, and the vaginal opening.

❦ **Vestibule:** The area within the inner lips, containing the urethra and vaginal openings.

❦ **Hymen:** Named after the Greek god of marriage, it is a thin membrane that covers the passageway into the vagina and is located about a third of the way in, with an opening in the middle to allow for menstrual blood to drain out. The hymen is a tissue left over from the end of the first trimester of embryonic life, when the vagina and urethra separated from each other as they were formed. In most girls the hymen wears away during physical activities such as riding a bicycle, running, jumping, climbing, doing gymnastics, or using tampons. By the time they reach adulthood, the majority of women will have only a few tags of hymen skin left, which cannot even be felt during penetration. However, some women will have an intact hymen, which is usually stretched out and eliminated ("broken") during first-time intercourse causing little pain and minimal bleeding that last less than a day. At times though, there will be an especially thick, rigid hymen that requires surgical removal—a simple medical procedure that takes just a few minutes. In rare situations, the hymen may be without an opening, a condition known as an "imperforate hymen," which is a medical emergency that necessitates surgery to cut it open and drain the menstrual blood that has been accumulating in the uterus and causing bloating, pain, etc. An imperforate hymen is usually diagnosed in teenage years when the adolescent experiences cyclic cramps, pelvic bloating, and pain but without passing any blood. Because it serves no purpose, the hymen never grows back once it is disintegrated. However, some women will choose to undergo a surgical procedure to repair or replace their hymen because of the cultural and religious meaning it has in defining virginity and the consummation of a marriage.

* **Pelvic Floor Diaphragm:** A sling-like structure that is made of supportive tissue and of muscles, stretching across the bottom of the pelvis from side to side and from front to back and creating a floor as if to prevent the content of the pelvis from falling out. The urethra, the vagina, and the rectal canal pass through this diaphragm on their way to the outside, which means that when the muscles of the pelvic floor diaphragm contract, they squeeze the three passages and make them narrower. The popular term for the pelvic floor diaphragm is the "PC muscle," referring to the Pubococcygeus muscle that is a part of this structure.

Of the three passages through the pelvic floor, the vagina is the opening all women with vaginismus feel is restricted, with common descriptions being either "I don't have a hole" or "Getting in is like hitting a wall." The anus and urethra do not tend to be perceived as constricted because the functions of voiding (urinating and defecating) usually continue in an uninterrupted manner, because the urethra is not involved in voluntary penetration, and because anal sex does not seem to be a sexual option for most vaginismus sufferers. However, since these openings are components of the pelvic floor structure, they are affected by the muscle spasm, although the severity and the specific symptomology will differ from one woman to the next.

We understand that women who suffer from vaginismus may not be comfortable touching themselves in order to feel the pelvic floor muscles. But, if you are comfortable, insert your index finger into your vagina as deep as the middle knuckle; while holding it still inside, tighten the vagina as if you are trying to resist urinating, or as if you are trying to hold back diarrhea from coming out. Keep your hips down and try to limit the tightening to the inside of the vagina/rectum only, without allowing the inner thighs, buttocks, or abdomen to participate. You should feel a squeeze around/in front of your finger—this is it!

However, you **should not feel bad** if you cannot touch yourself. You may be apprehensive or unsure of new experiences, or perhaps your body and mind have a worry or an upsetting story to tell about penetration. This is what vaginismus is all about.

We define vaginismus as an *involuntary, instantaneous* tightening (spasm) of the pelvic floor diaphragm. This spasm causes the openings in the female genitals to become constricted and makes penetration painful or impossible.

The medical literature mentions two types of vaginismus:

- **Primary:** When the woman has always had it.

- **Secondary:** Where the woman was able to have penetration but lost that ability because of a trauma, such as infection, injury, surgery, abuse, etc.

Based on our clinical experience and in order to remain within the scope of this book, we will discuss the condition as one—*vaginismus*—regardless of its onset, because the symptomology and the recovery process will follow the same general principles.

Another term that is important to introduce is dyspareunia: difficult or painful sexual intercourse. Vaginismus is one of several reasons for this condition; others include scar tissue following an episiotomy, decreased elasticity of the vaginal opening because of low estrogen, size incompatibility as when the man's penis is exceptionally larger than the woman's vaginal opening, etc., all discussed at length in a separate chapter that is devoted to this condition.

So why, you may ask, does my pelvic floor musculature tighten if I really want to insert a tampon or have penetration? And why can't I just relax and make it go away? The answer is: vaginismus happens as a protective response to stress, apprehension, or fear associated with penetration, and it is a natural function of our stress response mechanism, also known as the fight-or-flight response.

The Medical Explanation

Let us first describe, in simple terms, our nervous system, in order to understand the stress response mechanism and how to use it in a positive way.

The body's Central Nervous System contains the brain and spinal cord and it can be easily viewed as a main expressway with many exit ramps.

The Peripheral Nervous System is the network of exits and their continual roads off the main expressway. In anatomical terms, these would be the nerves from the spinal cord to the rest of the body. This system is further divided into other subsystems that may be easier to view as a diagram:

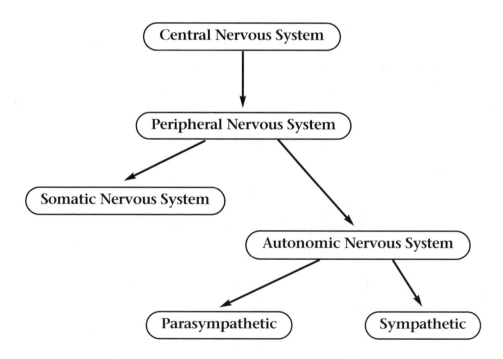

The **Somatic Nervous System** is responsible for the innervation of the skin, skeletal muscles, joints, and connective tissues (tendons, cartilage, etc.) and the senses (smell, vision, hearing, and taste).

The **Autonomic Nervous System** is responsible for the control of involuntary and visceral bodily functions such as cardiovascular (heart), respiratory (lungs, breathing), digestive, urinary, and reproductive. The Autonomic Nervous System also plays a key role in the body's response to rest and stress, through its two subsystems:

❦ The **Parasympathetic Nervous System,**
which is responsible for quieting the body and conserving energy by regulating "ordinary" functions such as rest and repose, sexual arousal, and feeding. This system is always in opposition to its twin system . . .

❦ The **Sympathetic Nervous System (SNS),**
which enables and activates the body for emergency by preparing the body to react under stress by activating the fight-or-flight response.

In other words, during each moment of our lives, we are utilizing the function of either the Parasympathetic Nervous System or the Sympathetic Nervous System (SNS), but never both at the same time; we are always either in a state of positive (e.g., calm, relaxed, or just plain "neutral"), or negative (e.g., stressed, upset, fearful, on guard, scared, etc.). One may view these two opposing systems as the checks and balances of the body and mind, providing the necessary hormones, chemicals, and physical functions of life in a balanced way.

It is within the protective nature of the SNS that we can find explanations to the overwhelming bodily reactions of panic and anxiety that are associated with vaginismus:

☞ The SNS is a fast, efficient system because the neurological impulses (the "on" switching) travel along very short neurons (the electrical wires in the nervous system), with a direct effect on glands (for producing chemicals necessary for action) and muscles (which carry out the action). In other words, the reaction is instantaneous, an important factor in panic and anxiety!

☞ The SNS, when activated, stimulates involuntary bodily reactions and movements (listed below) that are necessary for fighting or fleeing at times of danger, similar to an animal who reacts instantly (reflexively) when scared or startled. This powerful action by the body (without any intervention by the mind) often leads to the feeling of being "controlled," or "trapped," as in panic and anxiety. The truth is that this fight-or-flight reaction is a protective mechanism for when actual danger is present, or for when we need to take fast, immediate action, such as when we are involved in a car accident or if we trip and fall. Unfortunately, this protective mechanism can go awry, as in the case of vaginismus, when penetration is *perceived* as a negative, or is provoking existing fears.

The specific bodily reactions that are typical of the fight-or-flight response include:

- Stimulated sweat glands (for controlling body temperature that rises during fighting and/or fleeing).

- Constriction (narrowing) of peripheral blood vessels.

- Increased blood supply to skeletal muscles (to allow for fighting and/or fleeing).

- Dilated (opened) airways for efficient breathing during these efforts.

- Reduced blood flow to the abdomen (shutting down non-vital organs).

- Relaxed smooth (involuntary) muscles in the bladder.

- Released glucose (sugar) stored in the liver for increased energy.

If the need to fight or flee is to last for more than a few minutes, the SNS then activates another vital area called the Adrenal Medulla (a gland by each kidney), which releases additional hormones with the same effect on the above organs, but with a longer-lasting effect:

- Increased rate and force of contraction of the heart muscle.

- Constriction of blood vessels.

- Dilatation (opening) of bronchioles (airways).

🕊 Stimulation of fat metabolism to ensure continual energy and to prevent depletion of blood glucose (sugar).

🕊 Increased metabolic rate for a heightened state of alert.

🕊 Dilatation of the pupils, enabling better vision in low light.

🕊 Shutting down of non-vital organs such as the intestines.

Having read the above explanations, one might clearly admit that the body is a sophisticated machine that provides for rapid, efficient reactions in response to critical changes in life. It certainly makes sense that we need heightened state of alert at times of action, but not when we eat, sleep, relax, are intimate, etc.

Of all the above-mentioned reactions, the most upsetting feature is the rapid breathing, which has a frightening impact that leads to more stress and to an even more rapid, shallow breathing—a phenomenon called hyperventilation. But, as frightening as hyperventilation may be, including the associated feeling of faintness—one must remember that the body has a safety mechanism in place and it "knows" what to do when we breathe too fast.

Hyperventilation is defined as ventilation in excess of metabolic requirements (i.e., breathing is faster than the rate of production of carbon dioxide [CO_2], leading to losing too much of this vital gas [hypocapnia]). When hyperventilating, the tendency toward upper-chest breathing becomes more pronounced and biochemical imbalances occur (relative alkalosis of the bloodstream), which automatically produce a sense of apprehension and anxiety.

Hyperventilation is a normal response to oxygen deficiency (hypoxia), but is most commonly produced by emotional stress, anxiety, apprehension or fear. Typical symptoms include lightheadedness, dizziness, anxiety, superficial tingling in the extremities (arms and legs) and around the lips, muscle spasms, paleness, cold clammy skin, and in severe cases—unconsciousness.

Our nervous system monitors the balance of respiratory (breathing) gases—oxygen versus carbon dioxide—by adjusting the rate of respiration (breathing in and out). Therefore, hyperventilation is not a dangerous phenomenon, however scary it may seem. To help reversing hyperventilation, one may want to use a simple trick: breathing every second or third breath into a "brown paper bag" that is held tight around the mouth. The logic behind this simple trick is that the circulated air inside the bag has less oxygen, therefore increasing carbon dioxide intake and restoring the healthy balance of gases.

Putting it all together, the body has a natural defense mechanism—fight-or-flight response—that gets activated immediately upon stress and/or danger, may they be real or perceived, enabling the person to react in a reflexive, protective way. However, this protective reaction may become "conditioned" as a result of repeated fears or worries, causing the SNS to be either in a frequent or constant state of action, or be activated at the slightest hint of worry.

Consider the following from Lisa's diary:

I remember the moment very clearly. I was driving on the parkway, hit a bump in the road, and felt as if I was going to die. My heart started to race. I felt like I couldn't breathe. I began to perspire. I felt very nervous and started to tremble. I didn't realize until several months later that what I had experienced was a panic attack. Over the next few months, my life continued to proceed down a spiraling path of symptoms that led to an increasing fear. Everywhere I went I was surrounded by a strange array of symptoms including dizziness, trembling, racing heart, feelings of being unbalanced or falling down, and general feelings that something "bad" was going to happen. Every area of my life was beginning to suffer. I went from being a very independent and happy person who loved to travel and explore the world to a very frightened individual who lived each moment in fear—waiting for the next "bad" feeling to creep up on me. Needless to say, life, as I knew it, had ended. I couldn't see beyond the fear and the pain that was living in my mind and my body. While dealing with panic and anxiety attacks on a daily basis, I was also suffering from a different kind of pain. I was diagnosed with vaginismus. I had never heard this word before and would swear that someone had made it up. I knew that I was unable to have a gynecological exam, use a tampon, or have intercourse. I felt totally empty. I didn't know which way to turn or whom to seek help from.

How is it all related to vaginismus? The muscles of the pelvic floor are intimately related to the stress response mechanism in being predominantly innervated by the Sympathetic Nervous System! What we suggest by this fact is that the pelvic floor reacts at times of stress by tightening and squeezing the vagina, urethra, and anus. Since not all women suffer from vaginismus, for the pelvic floor to become such a stress zone, the woman must suffer from negative association regarding sex, penetration, body image, relationship, etc., some of the causes for this condition, which are discussed in the next chapter.

The following is from the diary of a former patient who experienced one of the most severe panic and anxiety attacks we have encountered during a treatment process. She named her essay "The Vaginismus Chronicles":

Being asked to write about vaginismus is a very hard thing to do, especially since I've spent the last ten years trying to pretend that nothing in my life was wrong. Now that I've been helped and have successfully recovered, I find the need to share my thoughts with others because there are still so many people who have never heard of it and shrug it off as being "all in your mind.

My husband and I have been married for eight years, and were together for three years before that day. As our relationship grew, we grew closer in other ways as well. Having both been raised as Catholics, we agreed that we would wait until our wedding night before having intercourse. Although we did do other things, our agreement was in place and neither of us knew what we were heading toward or how long it would be before we finally shared that ultimate act of intimacy.

Our wedding night was certainly an eye-opener, although we attributed it to being tired and stressed after all the rigors of the wedding day. However, once we were settled into our hotel, we found it wasn't going to be as simple as we had always assumed it would be. Our first night of trying left my husband frustrated and myself in tears, with a major migraine brewing. The next two weeks were pretty much the same. My husband, being a generous man, did not try to force the issue, and we went home feeling a huge letdown.

Over the years, things got progressively worse, although we did manage to have fun doing something my husband terms "outercourse." Doing that I managed to have orgasms, so I buried my head about the seriousness of the situation. Every once in a while, my husband would try to bring up the subject. Then I would become defensive and the result would be an argument. Looking back on it now, I can't believe that I was so wrapped up in myself and how it all made me feel, that I never really thought much about it from his point of view. But with the guilt that I was feeling, I knew that I had to do something, but I wasn't sure what and I wasn't ready to admit that there was a serious problem that I could not handle.

About three years ago, I took a tentative step in trying to rectify the situation. By now, my husband had made it clear that something needed to be done, and soon. One of my coworkers gave me the name of her gynecologist (his name shall never be repeated by me; more on that later) and I very shakily set up an appointment. Now, I had never, in my thirty years, been examined by anyone, so to say that I was nervous is to put it very mildly. I was terrified and he was not the understanding type. After being examined for all of three seconds (not that I really let him get that close), he stated that he knew what the problem was and told me that I needed a Hymenectomy. Finding out that I needed an operation was a scary prospect, but the thought of being "cured" overrode any fear I might be feeling (and there was plenty!).

After having the operation and being told that it was successful, I had to return to the doctor's office to make sure that everything had healed. But I found, to my chagrin, that nothing had changed and he still couldn't examine me. He pretty much brushed me off, and my husband and I left the office. Unfortunately, this situation did not help me in further investigating my problem. In fact, I really believed that it must be all in my head and that something psychologically was wrong. But I just buried my head and told my husband and myself that I could fix this myself. We did continue to try, but nothing changed and how could it, when I didn't even know what was wrong? Then suddenly last summer, a light began to glint at the end of our long, dark tunnel.

My husband was watching the later edition of the news one evening and saw a piece about something that sounded like what we were experiencing. Having knowledge of the Internet, he found information about it and even had a name for it: vaginismus. The next morning when I awoke, I was to find printed pages dealing with the subject and where to go for help. I'm ashamed to admit it, but I still refused to talk about it and was loath to even looking at the information. What if I needed another operation? Or an exam? I was scared to even admit that this could be my problem because then I'd have to fix it and I didn't know if I could face another doctor who would look at me as if I were a wacko.

It took me three months before I would agree to see anyone and even then, my husband was the one who had to make the appointment. I felt like I was walking to the guillotine. I have to admit that I didn't speak much and was highly suspicious of what I heard, but after the two hours were over, I found myself agreeing to come back. I think what really pushed me to my decision was hearing my husband admit that after my operation, while I was in the recovery room, the doctor came out and told him that if he would be "more of a man," there would be no problem! Talk about anger strengthening you to do things you could not ordinarily do!

Returning to the office for my first solo visit was not too bad. I knew we were going to talk, but I never imagined that the therapy part (which involved looking, and later on, touching) would begin so soon. I was not thrilled with this, but I gritted my teeth, determined to suffer through it. When we reached the "inserting" stage, however, I found that I was no longer in control. Although both clinicians were very kind and understanding, they also let me know that they would not let me get away with panicking and refusing to do what I needed to do to get better. To me, this was unheard of; Whenever I got upset at home, my husband would back off. This was not the case here. At one point, I even found out that I was no longer in control in terms of my body. The first time that a finger was inserted,

I had a massive panic attack and my body went into shock. I began to hyperventilate, couldn't feel my fingers, and became dizzy. I was given a bag to breathe into, and some really sweet tea to relieve the dizziness. When I finally regained control of myself, we spoke and then we tried it again! I was still very agitated, but I did not panic, and that is when I knew that I could regain control of my life.

I won't lie and say that it was a piece of cake after that first encounter with my fear. I questioned whether I would return for my next scheduled session. But somehow, the car always made the trip and I found support and encouragement at the end of the journey. I went for two hours twice a week, and although I was really scared at first, it got easier as I went along. Then suddenly, it was December and my husband was asked to come in and discuss intercourse. Neither of us could believe that we were so close to achieving our goal, but as we sat and listened, we realized that the time had come to put the years of frustration behind us.

We went away to a bed-and-breakfast that weekend. Remaining calm, we once again attempted to consummate our relationship and I cannot begin to explain the relief and the freedom we felt from the weight that had been hanging around our necks for the past ten years. I think the first words that I uttered were,"I'm not a virgin any more." Then we laughed and cried. Since that morning in December, I feel like a totally different person. I can look at my friends who have children and honestly say that that could be me someday soon. Although my husband and I have a very strong relationship, something more has been added to it and I think we both walk with a bit more confidence in our steps. When I think of all the years that I lived in fear and in agony of never being "normal," I could kick myself for not having the courage to do more and seek out people who could help me. I am just fortunate that I finally did connect with people who could guide me through my fears and show me that there is a whole other world out there that I had been keeping myself hidden from and that other people like me are out there, too, waiting for someone to help them.

In summary, vaginismus is the instantaneous, involuntary tightening of the pelvic floor muscles in anticipation of penetration. This reaction will occur if penetration is perceived as dangerous, frightening, or upsetting, making the body scream out loud, "NO ENTRY!"

Vaginismus may be provoked either through the body by a touch or an attempted penetration, or from the mind by either thinking about penetration or by remembering upsetting or traumatic past experiences. Once such an association is established, it becomes a conditioned response and gets easily reactivated every time penetration is mentioned or attempted, sending the woman into a distressing body-mind experience. Most importantly, in being involuntary in nature, vaginismus does not respond to suggestions such as "relax," "don't think about it," "it will go away," "have a drink," "just do it," "take antianxiety medications"—common suggestions women are given by frustrated doctors and therapists.

The Functional Outcome

There are two common denominators uniting all women who suffer from vaginismus: the inability or difficulty with vaginal penetration, and the associated emotional stress. The level and severity of each may vary from one woman to another, which explains the differences in the symptomology between patients.

The pelvic floor muscles that we discussed above are known to have four biological functions that are well defined in the medical literature, and are quite clear to any healthcare provider:

- ❧ A mechanical support to the urethra, the vagina, and the anus.

- ❧ A sphincter enhancement to ensure urinary and fecal continence.

- ❧ A necessary component for micturation (urinating) and defecation.

- ❧ A vital component of the sexual response mechanism—contracting rapidly and bringing about orgasm.

The fifth function, one that we have identified in our work with vaginismus, is that of a defense mechanism, by virtue of its SNS innervation as described above and the "NO ENTRY!" reaction. Unfortunately, the functional implications of this psychophysical reaction are slow to be recognized and accepted by healthcare professionals, which is the main reason behind the limited understanding of the condition and the lack of a predictable, successful treatment approach.

In addition to a better understanding of the intimate association between the SNS and the pelvic floor, one must also appreciate the varied penetrations that typify a woman's existence, which we coined **The Five Penetrations of Life.** We strongly believe that every woman should have the ability to experience these basic vaginal penetrations, without any difficulty, and to choose to engage in any or all of them as per her own lifestyle:

☞ Finger.

☞ Tampon.

☞ Applicator (for inserting medication into the vagina).

☞ Pelvic exam.

☞ Intercourse.

Since not all women suffer from vaginismus in the same way, they will not suffer from the same limitations; that is, they may be able to have some of **The Five Penetrations of Life** available but not all of them. Here are typical variations that we have seen in our practice:

☞ Able to use tampons and have a finger inserted, but nothing else.

☞ Able to have a pelvic exam, use tampons, and insert an applicator, but unable to have intercourse. Any attempt at intercourse is met with anxiety.

☞ Able to have a pelvic exam despite a great deal of pain and anxiety, yet unable to have any other penetration.

❦ Able to have intercourse despite severe pain and distress.

❦ Unable to have penetration of any kind. Any attempt is met with severe panic and anxiety.

❦ Resistant to any touch in the area, including the inner thighs, the abdomen, and the pubic hair.

We prefer to view the genitals and the pelvic floor as an "emotional whole," instead of just as a receptacle for penetrative activities. This body-mind connection is the reason why vaginismus will often include additional difficulties that are associated with any or all of the following activities:

❦ Looking at own genitals.

❦ Touching own genitals (hygiene care, shaving, wiping after urination, etc.).

❦ Masturbation (clitoral stimulation).

❦ Receiving manual and/or oral sex from partner.

❦ Reaching orgasm.

❦ Perceiving the area as numb or detached from the rest of the body.

There seems to be a sense of estrangement from the body that is common to vaginismus sufferers, be it apprehension because of lack of knowledge, resentment, or even hate of "those parts that betrayed me." This estrangement brings along emotional manifestations that aid in furthering the confusion experienced by the patient and by the healthcare professional regarding the nature of the condition and the direction of intervention. Statements we commonly hear from patients include "I believe they think I am making this up," "What if I don't do it (sex) right?" or "The doctor told me to get over it and insert something into my vagina, but I cannot." A repeated statement is that of "I am worried that (my partner, the doctor) will look at my genitals and feel disgusted." These feelings represent the typical SNS reactions most visible at times of either attempted pelvic exam or intercourse: sweating, shaking, urinary urgency, nervousness, nausea, stomachaches, closing legs tight, general body tightening, flatulence (passing gas), holding breath, grasping on to bed or wall or clutching fists tight, vocal reactions (e.g., crying, begging to stop, screaming, etc.), pushing away, breaking out in hives, etc. Of course, not all women will respond in the same way, but each will experience at least some of these reactions, if not all of them. Overall, the emotional stress may range from minimal apprehension and nervousness to severe anxiety and/or a panic attack, and even to flashbacks in cases of traumatic experiences in the past. While remembering that every woman will have a different emotional pattern, the following is a quick summary of the emotional breakdowns that characterize vaginismus:

- Self-blame, shame, and guilt.

- Accepting pain as an inseparable part of life, yet at the same time fearing and avoiding it.

- Depression.

🐾 Living in secrecy.

🐾 Frustration, desperation.

🐾 Anger at the medical field for dismissing the magnitude of the problem and/or for placing the blame on the woman who suffers.

🐾 Avoidance (of intimacy, of relationships, etc.)

🐾 Breakdown of intimacy, relationships, marriages.

🐾 Body shut-down (discussed in detail in a separate chapter).

🐾 Sexual dysfunction.

🐾 Dissociation.

The wall of silence that surrounds vaginismus and the limited resources for treatment are the cause behind the prime belief of every sufferer: "I am the *only* one who has it," a devastating feeling that compounds the already complex makeup of the condition.

The following testimonial, written for this book by one of our former patients, summarizes the devastating effect of vaginismus:

> *When my husband and I were just dating, we decided to wait until we were married to have intercourse. My husband was also a virgin. We spoke often about how wonderful it would be to consummate our marriage on our wedding night: to begin this sexual journey together. Well, it didn't quite work out that way. We began our marriage with a different journey—*

one that began with frustrations and anxiety that eventually evolved into education, communication, and understanding.

About four months before we were married, I decided to go to the gynecologist for birth control pills. At twenty-five years old, I had been able to avoid going to the gynecologist despite pressure from my mother as well as from my primary care doctor. I had heard various things about going to a gynecologist— all of them very negative. I did not want to go. After reading on the Internet what to expect at a gynecological visit, I was very nervous about having something inserted into my vagina. I was making myself sick thinking about the appointment. Despite what I read, I didn't know what to expect. I had never had anything inserted. I never used tampons; whenever my husband tried to insert his finger, I wouldn't let him; and I never explored my own body. As long as everything worked properly, I didn't think about it.

As you can imagine, the gynecologist's visit was not very successful. When she tried to insert the speculum, I kept moving back. My whole body was tense. The doctor brought in a nurse who tried to help me relax. Nothing helped. Even when she tried to examine the outer lips, I was incredibly tense. The doctor said that she would not try the speculum again but she would have to try and insert her finger in order to make sure that nothing was physically wrong. She was barely able to insert her finger and at this point I was in pain and crying. I wanted to leave as quickly as possible. After the exam, she told me not to worry about it; it would be better after I'd had intercourse. She also encouraged me to use tampons. She gave me the prescription for the Pill and I left.

I remember speaking to my husband after the appointment. Despite what the doctor had told me, I felt abnormal—this doesn't happen to anyone else! My friends had all been to the gynecologist without a problem. What was wrong with me? After my husband and I discussed it, we felt a little better knowing that everything would be better once we had intercourse.

Needless to say, our wedding night was not the magical night that we had envisioned. When my husband tried to penetrate, it was extremely painful. It just didn't feel right. Something was wrong. He tried to comfort me but we both didn't understand why I was feeling so much pain. Again, I thought, "This is such a natural process for other people, why are we having so much trouble?" We comforted ourselves by saying it was our first try and it was bound to be painful. Next time would be better.

During our honeymoon, we tried many times— hoping that with practice, it would not be so painful. We came up with many theories during this time about why this was happening. We thought that my hymen was fully intact or maybe the vaginal opening was being stretched and that was why it was so painful. But we were convinced that we should keep trying. We even thought that it was getting better. But we still weren't sure if we were actually having intercourse. Since we were both virgins, we didn't know what it was supposed to feel like. Now when I look back on this situation, it always makes me laugh. I know now that we were not having intercourse but our lack of knowledge and our desire to feel normal made us want to believe that we were.

Our first months of marriage were very happy; except for our sexual lives. I smiled through all the jokes about the "honeymoon stage." No one but my husband knew about this struggle. I did not feel comfortable speaking to anyone about this—even my closest friends. I didn't want anyone to know. Who could understand a newly married couple not having intercourse? So I kept up the persona that we were everything that newlyweds should be. I couldn't speak to anyone about it. It was too embarrassing.

Eventually, it was time again to visit the gynecologist for my annual visit. I knew that I had to tell the doctor about the trouble that I was having, but I was still afraid to go to the appointment. A couple of weeks before the appointment, I thought it would be best to try and use tampons before the appointment. I thought that if I was able to use tampons, I would be able to deal with the speculum. Once I got my period, I tried every night to insert a tampon. I was able to insert the tampon halfway. Trying to push the tampon further was like trying to push it through a brick wall. It wasn't budging. Usually these attempts would leave me in tears. WHAT WAS WRONG WITH ME? Everyone uses tampons. Why can't I do this? The feelings of inadequacy were sharpened. I thought that there must be something physically wrong with me. I told my husband over and over that I felt like a "freak." Thankfully, I have been blessed with an amazingly patient husband who struggled through this time with me and repeatedly told me that I was okay.

I knew that I had to go back to the gynecologist since the entire situation seemed to be getting worse!

I started the visit by asking to speak to the doctor in her office first. I told her about all of the difficulties that I was experiencing with the tampons and with intercourse. She asked me if I would be okay to try the Pap smear test and I agreed. Again, it was unsuccessful. Now when I look back on the situation, she could have tried a hundred times. It wouldn't have worked. She assured me that we would work through the situation and she would find someone to help me. She called me back later that day to give me the number of the Women's Therapy Center that a physical therapist had told her about. She told me that they would be able to treat my problem and help me to understand what was going on. I was a little skeptical about this center; but after reading the testimonials on the Website, I was comforted and hopeful. There were other people out in the world who were having the same problem. I couldn't believe it! I was very nervous about the treatment process but I felt that this was my last resort.

After my first meeting, I practically skipped out of the office. This "thing" that I had been suffering with was "vaginismus." They told me three things that I needed to hear: 1) This is very common; 2) There are other people like you in the same situation; and 3) Vaginismus can be cured. These statements were very important to me. They made me hopeful that one day I would be able to overcome this condition and be a normal, sexually active adult!

Through the treatment process, I began to understand that my lack of knowledge about my own body and sexuality contributed to my fear and anxiety. Through the bodywork and education, I began to gain an understanding about my own body. I began to see that there was nothing to be feared about intercourse or a gynecological exam. I also began to feel like I had ownership over my body; that it was okay to explore my own body and sexuality.

Eventually, my husband and I were able to have intercourse. At first, it was mechanical, but with practice, it has become a wonderful part of our marriage. It is wonderful to be able to connect with him in this way and to finally feel like a newlywed.

My final victory, of course, was going back to the gynecologist for an exam. She was shocked and amazed at how relaxed I was compared to my other visits. She was able to perform the exam without any problems.

Ten months after getting married, my husband and I have happily settled into the honeymoon stage; and this time, it's exactly as we had imagined!

CHAPTER FIVE

Vaginismus Statistics

How prevalent is vaginismus? How many women suffer from it in the United States and worldwide? What is the typical vaginismus patient like? Is there a permanent cure? How long does the treatment process take? I was never abused, so how come I have vaginismus?

Good questions . . . that have remained unanswered because vaginismus is a "private pain" problem: Shame and feelings of inadequacy usually lead to keeping it a secret, instead of discussing it openly, on route to finding answers. The medical and mental health professions have also been frustrated in their struggles to provide a clear, predictable treatment approach, adding to the silence and resignation that sufferers are forced to accept.

The media has been an instrumental force for defining preferred sexual looks and sexual behaviors, highlighting the gap between reality and fantasy. The average person is far from the image and sexual practice that are presented by the media, adding to the sexual pressure between men and women, and making those who "do not look sexy or act sexy," feel like a failure.

Our clinical and professional experience reinforces the fact that there are many women worldwide who suffer from this condition . . . in silence. We have also learned that some cultures and certain religions view womanhood, courtship, marriage, and sexuality in ways that limit the woman's sexual choices, further deepening the gap between suffering in silence and speaking up.

As part of our ongoing campaign to bring vaginismus into the open, we have been keeping careful records of inquiries and treatments rendered at our private practice, gathering data that is sufficient for presenting the following vaginismus profile. Although these outcomes have been consistent in the past few years, the reader is nevertheless urged to visit our Website for the most recent update [**www.womentc.com**].

What is the family status of the vaginismus patient?

- 🐚 Forty-seven percent are either single or dating.

- 🐚 Fifty-three percent are married, anywhere from a few months to over thirty years.

What is the age of the typical vaginismus patient?

🍂 Eighteen percent are under the age of twenty-five. This figure could be much higher if the condition were to be better understood and properly diagnosed at an earlier age.

🍂 Fifty-three percent are between the ages of twenty-six to thirty-five, the age group when most women become sexually active and get married, realizing the problem of vaginismus.

🍂 Twenty percent are between the ages of thirty-six to fifty, mostly including women who married late in life or those who have been in unconsummated marriages for many years, suffering in silence before seeking help.

🍂 Nine percent are over the age of fifty-one.

Do educated women suffer from vaginismus?

Vaginismus is a fearful reaction to penetration. It is an inner feeling shared by women regardless of educational level or intelligence—it is a condition without boundaries! In our statistical data:

🍂 Eighty-two percent are college graduates/professionals.

🍂 None percent are students (entry level to doctoral degrees).

🍂 Nine percent are homemakers.

Is abuse the most common cause for vaginismus?

Not at all. Only 29 percent of our database experienced abuse, whether verbal, emotional, physical, sexual, or rape. In other words, over two-thirds *never* experienced any abuse, which is contrary to beliefs strongly held by many professionals!

What is the cure rate of our treatment program?

Ninety-five percent. Our body-mind treatment approach is a well-defined concept with a proven high success rate. The other 5 percent that did not complete the process include women who never returned past the introductory appointment because of fear of being touched, women who couldn't afford the treatment, women who relocated, and a few women whose husbands denied them the option of treatment (victims of domestic violence). In other words, **those who stayed with the treatment process completed it successfully.**

Will vaginismus come back once cured?

No. The treatment process ensures a cure for life, because it removes the need to have the body speak for the mind about the fear of penetration. The treatment process takes the woman through penetrations in a guided, safe, painless way, eliminating the need for the fight-or-flight reaction and for pelvic floor muscle spasms. Once cured, the condition will never return regardless of situations such as a new partner, pregnancy, childbirth, or surgery.

What is the average length of treatment?

Seventeen hours, with treatment frequency varying from one to four hours per week, depending on the particular needs of each patient. Women who live locally are treated twice weekly, an ideal time frame that allows for steady intervention with integration time between sessions. Women who come to us from out-of-town are treated up to four hours daily for the duration of their stay, for an average total of thirty to thirty-six hours. Although they are cured faster (within two weeks), they require more treatment hours than average because of the concentrated nature of their process, the reduced restitution time between sessions. Overall, the success rate stands the same for locals and for out-of-towners—ninety-five percent.

How prevalent is vaginismus? I never heard of it before.

The actual numbers of vaginismus sufferers in the general population are hard to come by due to the veil of secrecy and embarrassment that surrounds the condition. Most gynecologists that we interviewed claimed that not one of their patients suffered from vaginismus, only to realize otherwise once they either became familiar with the condition, or assigned a (female) nurse to the role of taking detailed sexual history. Since there is a need for some estimate of prevalence, one may want to look at the activity in our vaginismus Website (inquiries are from the United States as well as worldwide):

- 🐚 In August 1999, we received 500 inquiries.

- 🐚 By January 2000, this number grew to 1,050.

- 🐚 By late 2000, we averaged over 1,730 inquiries every month.

- 🐚 Since January 2001, we have been averaging well over 2,000 inquiries each month!

Simple arithmetic suggests that over thirty-eight thousand people contacted us about vaginismus in a two-year span! And the numbers continue to grow every day.

CHAPTER SIX

Is There a Cure for Vaginismus?

Allie, My Story . . .

*T*he first time I tried to have sex, I was hit with the sense that something was terribly wrong. I was surprised and disappointed and so confused at the fact that I just couldn't seem to relax and although I had heard that being anxious the first time is normal, I felt it was bigger than that. My heart started racing and I felt this darkness begin to close in on me, and an intense pain overtook my body, all of which escalated with every try after that for years to come.

I was sixteen and being the only one of my friends to have a boyfriend during that time, I'd have unending inquiries about my sex life but I couldn't seem to tell anyone about the problem. I was so embarrassed and confused and being so young, I had no idea how to broach a subject like this with anyone. I had thoughts that this must be happening because I wasn't supposed to have sex. Premarital sex was something I remember hearing was wrong as a child, and me, being one of those kids that follows the rules, thought maybe I wasn't allowing myself to be sexual. Was I deeply religious on a subconscious level? Here I had thought I made a clear decision that I was ready with my boyfriend of one year. Ok, maybe it was just that it was my first time, I thought. But for the next ten years, every time I tried to have sex, to use a tampon, or to have an exam, it would create a panic that would leave me motionless.

When my friends asked, I told them I hadn't done it yet and their reactions left a startling impact on me. Their shock and references to me as a prude seemed to put me on constant guard, always on the lookout for the questions to begin. When I left home for college, I found the fear of someone finding out my secret grew even more intense. I closed myself off from the new friends I was making, giving them only a glimpse, just the very surface, so no one would get too close and ask me the questions I dreaded to hear.

Moments of fun seemed to dull with this constant weight I was carrying. What if someone found out? What would they think of me? I felt like a failure as a human being, and especially as a woman. As sex began showing up everywhere, it seemed every reference, every sign, every movie, and every song made me feel different. I couldn't do what everybody else in the world was able to.

Relationships with boyfriends over these years left me feeling incredibly inadequate. I began to run away from anyone I was interested in because I couldn't stand the thought of having to explain. My self-confidence was diminishing.

My sophomore year at college, I was home on a break and decided in a moment of strength to try yet again to use a tampon, something I'd tried many times over the years. Unlike any other try before, this time I got it inside me! But I suffered from a panic attack so severe I passed out, waking up moments later on the floor. It was then that I decided to talk about it for the first time ever in my life. I went to see the school psychologist, who told me what I had was called vaginismus. When she said these words, I felt shocked that there was a name for my demon secret. I ran to the library and sat between the bookshelves with a pile of sexual health books and read for the first time about this condition that had grabbed hold of my life and turned it inside out. I cried as each case was described and every symptom mirrored my own and I felt this intense sense that I was no longer alone.

Finding the cure for me would be another few years away. I saw gynecologists who had never heard the word vaginismus, I saw a psychologist who taught me relaxation techniques, I saw a specialist who told me to do Kegel exercises, and I was given dilators and told to go home and put them inside me. Nothing worked. With every doctor I visited, I got a strange sense that they didn't believe me. If I had felt like a failure before, I felt so much worse then. These doctors seemed to think I was making this up, that every time I attempted to put anything into my vagina I didn't feel as if a knife was being twisted around inside me. If they thought this was in my head, maybe it was. Was I crazy? I couldn't tell what was real, what was true, how I felt anymore. I began doubting every feeling and thought I had. Suddenly the world seemed like a dark, lonely place and I wasn't sure where I fit in. This was the furthest cry from my pre-vaginismus days.

I think vaginismus victims lose their spirit. Growing up I felt a spark inside me and a huge passion for life. Through the years of suffering with vaginismus, however, I felt my flame go out. It seemed to be replaced by a sadness that I felt deep within. If you've ever met anyone with sadness that you can see in their eyes, that is the only way for me to describe it. I was afraid to look people in the eyes because I thought they would see inside at all the sadness I felt.

I was flipping through an issue of Glamour *magazine a few months ago and the headline, "I Couldn't Have Sex—At All," flew off the page at me. This was how I learned about the Women's Therapy Center and I gave them a call the next day. The first appointment I wasn't touched physically, but I was told about this condition and I discussed with them my particular case, the things I had gone through, my feelings about sex and about getting treatment. I remember thinking, these women don't know what they're in for with me, I will be different from the rest and with me it won't work.*

That first day of bodywork was difficult and scary but not nearly as bad as I anticipated. For the first time, I had to look at myself and feel myself and it was a challenge to say the least. But in that same appointment, I got the first spacer inside me. I felt my body glow when this happened, and the smile on my face was one of pure joy, something I remembered feeling sometime in the past but I hadn't felt in so long. The next appointment and with every appointment that followed, I would progress with a larger spacer and then an applicator and a tampon and a speculum. As every day passed while I was in treatment, I felt stronger, I felt empowered. When I did my homework at night, as difficult as it seemed to be at first, the feeling of success that overcame me while I conquered this demon was extraordinary. I felt renewed.

Vaginismus treatment is like a course in sexuality, and I feel so enlightened from having gone through this. This treatment was a lesson in sex, and in being comfortable with my body and dealing with the pain that had plagued me for so long. When I asked Ditza and Ross about this pain, what they told me made perfect sense and gave me all the knowledge I needed to get through. They said to accept that pain, and work right next to it, work right through it, and then it will diminish. I think that many of us believe when we feel pain, it means something must be wrong with our bodies, but they assured me that it was just a reaction to feeling a different sensation, something I was not yet used to. With that in mind, I felt powerful over the pain and instead of it ruling me, I was ruling it. I was in control for the first time, and from now on for the rest of my life.

79

It is also a lesson in self-perception. I realize that for all those years I'd been placing all of my self-worth on the fact that I was unable to have sex. I realize now that vaginismus is a medical problem, and just as any other medical ailment, there should be no shame in it. I have every right to feel proud of myself and happy and to love myself, vaginismus or not. Vaginismus does not lessen my value as a human being. I realize that now.

I have spoken to a few women who suffer from vaginismus since beginning treatment and every story I hear amazes me. I've met women just like me, suffering in silence and afraid to open up to anyone. I can see the same exact sadness in their eyes that I tried to hide in my own. All I want them to know is that there is a cure and their lives will change and their true selves are about to be rediscovered once they go through this treatment.

I believe that things happen for a reason and maybe there was a master plan for me having had vaginismus. The treatment has taught me so much about myself and about the things I can overcome. Before being cured, I saw no way out, I didn't have a light at the end of this tunnel, so the fact that I've overcome this makes me feel like I can do anything in this world! I have this respect for myself that I've never had before. Since finishing, I feel at peace. I feel content and confident and I no longer need to search for approval from others or most importantly from myself. Now, I find myself talking more and laughing constantly and trusting the person I am. What can I say, I'm so happy! This has changed my life, and I found that little girl that had lost her way.

CHAPTER SEVEN

Understanding Dyspareunia

*F*emale dyspareunia (dys•pa•reu•nia) means difficult or painful sexual intercourse. Although the condition is present in both sexes, it is far more common in women, where it is being described as pain with initial penetration, while thrusting, or after intercourse.

I never understood why tampons were so painful when everyone can use them just fine . . . Intercourse? I expected pain the first time, but it keeps being painful every time, from the moment he begins to penetrate until he is done. Although we have two kids, I am reluctant to engage in intercourse and still cannot use tampons. Gynecologic exams are also painful, and the doctor does not know what is the problem.

Definition

Dyspareunia is defined by dividing the presenting symptomology into three categories: *onset, frequency,* and *location.*

- ☜ **Onset** asks about the start of the problem: Has it been there since the first time intercourse was attempted (primary, or lifelong dyspareunia), or did it start after a period of having normal intercourse (secondary, or acquired dyspareunia)?

- ☜ **Frequency** examines whether the problem occurs with all partners and in all penetrative situations (complete, or generalized dyspareunia), or only at times, with certain partners, in certain positions, or because of certain circumstances (situational dyspareunia).

- ☜ **Location** describes whether the pain is upon initial penetration at the vaginal opening (insertional, or superficial dyspareunia), or during thrusting and at full penetration (deep dyspareunia).

Putting it all together, since the condition may present itself in different combinations, a thorough assessment is imperative in order to identify the particular type of dyspareunia the woman has. Typical variations may include:

- **Primary, situational, deep:** Thrusting always hurts while the woman is in the missionary position; other positions are okay.

- **Secondary, situational, insertional:** Experiences pain with current partner upon beginning of penetration, goes away as soon as the man's penis is halfway in; never happened with prior partners; pain is not as bad during menstrual cycle.

- **Primary, complete, superficial, and deep:** Has always had the problem, with all partners, in all positions, throughout the sexual act.

- **Secondary, complete, superficial:** Initial penetration has been painful since gynecologic surgery regardless of lubrication or sex position.

Symptomology

Women rarely seek medical assistance to discuss sexual difficulties, a fact that makes it impossible to assess the prevalence of dyspareunia (and vaginismus for that matter). The two main reasons behind this reluctance are women's tendency to accept pain as an inevitable part of intercourse, and their worry that the clinician will ridicule them or dismiss their complaints as "being crazy." On the other hand, the sad truth is that not all clinicians are attuned to the nature or presence of this condition, nor are they comfortable in discussing such intimate matters with their patients. As a matter of fact, most are reluctant to include sexual history and sexual dysfunctions as part of their screening process. The end result is that dyspareunia and vaginismus maintain a secretive, puzzling place in the professional and personal arenas.

The symptomology, though, is quite clear as the body expresses its difficulties in certain ways that are common to all sufferers. The following is a comprehensive list of the pain that is associated with the condition, with location extending from the external genitals to deep within the pelvis. Naturally, the specific symptomology of each woman will vary, depending on the type of dyspareunia she has:

- Superficial vulvar pain or tenderness.

- Vulvar itching, burning, or stinging.

- Pain or pressure behind the pubic bone.

- Pain at vaginal opening upon initial entry.

- The sensation of being "torn" at the vaginal entry.

- Mid-vaginal pain such as burning, sharp, searing or cramping.

- Vaginal dryness, friction, and irritation.

- Deep pain with thrusting, as if "something is being bumped into."

- Urinary burning and urgency.

- Pain with orgasm (if the woman was aroused to completion).

Although intercourse tends to be perceived as a sexually-arousing activity to a woman, the truth is far from that. The majority of women do not reach orgasm by way of vaginal penetration, but rather through clitoral stimulation with vaginal penetration being an added pleasure during the arousal process. The importance of orgasm varies in women, ranging from being an extremely important part of every sexual encounter, to being a desired outcome but not a necessary one, whereas emotional satisfaction is always mandatory. Therefore, dyspareunia may never present itself as painful orgasms if the woman reaches her sexual satisfaction in other ways than through vaginal intercourse.

Causes

I found intercourse painful. I never felt "elastic" enough, vaginally speaking, to comfortably accommodate his penis regardless of ample artificial lubrication. During insertion and penetration, I found it almost impossible to concentrate on what was happening because I felt the pressing urge to urinate. Or was terrified I would. Since my female parts were all present and undamaged, my doctor surmised that the problem was "in my head." This, unfortunately, reaffirmed my belief that I was just ABNORMAL. I felt despair as I pondered why I just couldn't be, or feel how I so desperately wanted to, like everybody else.

Pain with intercourse can be caused by a wide variety of reasons. This may complicate the diagnostic process of dyspareunia if the clinician is not knowledgeable about the condition, nor has the necessary patience to sort out the intricate body and mind manifestations that the woman may present. However, a careful assessment can usually identify the exact cause for the problem, making the treatment planning a simpler matter.

In an effort to present a descriptive summary of the causes for dyspareunia, the following categories were created for the sake of simplicity: medical causes, physical causes, functional causes, and psychophysical causes. A more detailed explanation of the anatomy of the female genitals is presented in a separate chapter, "What Is Vaginismus?"

Medical causes include:

- 🐚 Vaginal infections.

- 🐚 Dermatological conditions such as vulvar dystrophies (i.e. squamous hyperplasia or lichen sclerosis).

- 🐚 Pelvic disorders such as infections, cysts, uterine fibroids, endometriosis, chronic inflammatory disease, tumors, abnormalities of the cervix or the uterus.

- 🐚 Sexually transmitted diseases, such as herpes simplex virus that causes painful blisters, ulcerations, or fissures. The following is from a twenty-five-year-old married patient who stopped having intercourse several months before coming to us. She told us that she never had a problem before, but now intercourse is extremely painful and she no longer try to do it. *The problem started eighteen months ago when a cold sore on my husband's lip infected my genitals, giving me great pain. It was a very traumatic event for me and when the doctor was quite cold about it, he made me feel even worse. By now, although the sore is long healed, I am so worried about pain that I would not even attempt intercourse.*

🐝 Gastrointestinal disorders, such as irritable bowl syndrome, chronic constipation, diverticular disease, or hemorrhoids, where intercourse causes the penis to push on the intestines and cause pain. Also included in this cause are women who suffer from fecal incontinence (the accidental release of gas or feces) and who are afraid to lose control during intercourse.

🐝 Disorders of the urethra (i.e., cystitis), bladder (i.e., interstitial cystitis, which is pain upon filling of the bladder with urine), and anus.

🐝 Vulvar disorders, such as vulvitis (irritation of the vulva), vulvodynia (painful vulva), or vestibulitis (chronic inflammation of the vestibular structures).

🐝 Radiation therapy to the pelvis.

🐝 Estrogen deficiency, causing atrophic vaginitis (the thinning out and diminished elasticity of the vagina), impaired vaginal lubrication, diminished sexual arousal, etc. Estrogen deficiency is commonly the result of aging (menopause), radical hysterectomy (surgical menopause due to the removal of the ovaries), chronic hormonal deficiencies, etc.

☞ Diabetes, which may lead to fungal infections, itching, urinary tract infections because of nerve damage to the bladder (autonomic neuropathy), etc.

☞ Irritation or infection of the clitoris.

Physical causes include:

☞ Scars, adhesions, alterations, or neuropathy (nerve irritations) from procedures such as vaginal delivery, episiotomy, hysterectomy, cesarean section, urinary or orthopedic repairs, and from injuries to the groin or pelvis.

☞ Structural limitations, such as congenitally shortened vagina, retroverted (tipped) or prolapsed (dropped) uterus, or congenitally malformed vagina.

☞ Hymenal ring rigidity (resistant to stretch)— more about this topic in the chapter titled "Misconceptions about Treating Vaginismus."

☞ Physical incompatibility, as when the male's penis is much longer and/or thicker than average and cannot be accommodated by the female vagina, or if he has a penile deformity (such as Peyronie's disease, or a deviated penis) that makes vaginal penetration quite difficult.

🦢 A scrape or a small cut at the entrance to the vagina that is painful to touch and stretch as in penetration.

Functional causes include:

🦢 Excessive vulvar and/or vaginal irritation because of rough hygiene (i.e., deep rubbing), use of abrasive agents, ill-fitting sanitary pads, very tight clothing that cause chafing, certain sports that cause friction irritation (e.g., cycling, horseback riding, etc.), and substance sensitivity or allergy to chemicals in soap, feminine hygiene products, douches, contraceptive agents, foods, medications, etc.

🦢 Inadequate vaginal lubrication, which may be caused by hormonal changes (i.e., insufficient estrogen), certain drugs that have a drying effect (i.e., antihistamines for allergy, certain tranquilizers, medications for high blood pressure, and marijuana), insufficient hydration (not drinking enough), chemotherapy, chlorine from swimming pools, excessive hygiene practice, emotional stress, fear of penetration, and, in the case of sexual intimacy, insufficient stimulation/foreplay or just plain lack of interest in the activity.

🦢 Alteration of the vulva's ecosystem, described in further detail in the chapter titled "The Diagnosis and Symptoms of Vaginismus." Generally speaking, it refers to the interruption of the balance between the "good" and "bad" bacteria that live in the vaginal canal and which act as a protective mechanism against irritation and infections. This delicate balance may be adversely affected by repeated use of antibiotics, ingesting a diet rich in sugars and carbohydrates, prolonged exposure to warm and moist conditions (such as wearing a wet bathing suit for many hours on a hot day), infrequent change of bloody sanitary pads during menstruation, or a rise in estrogen levels. Forced or insistent penetration often results in vaginal chafing, contusions, or infections, further altering the ecosystem toward proliferation of undesirable bacteria rather than keeping a balance with the protective acid-loving lactobacillus, bifidus, and acidophilus.

Psychophysical causes include:

🍃 Postpartum (the weeks or even months after giving birth) is a time of transformation for a woman, characterized by hormonal and biological events that restore the body to pre-pregnancy state; physical mending of episiotomy or cesarean section; and adjusting to new responsibilities with a demanding daily schedule, etc. For most women, this is a period that combines healing with happiness. However, it can also be a traumatic period, as was the case with this twenty-nine-year-old woman who had her first baby: *The delivery was complicated; the baby was in intensive care for one week, and I suffered a separated pubic symphysis (pubic bone) that required the use of a wheelchair for several days before being able to walk with a cane while wearing a support band. Now, nearly one year later, I am completely healed, and the baby is fine and normal. However, I still refuse to even consider having intercourse, being petrified of any pain in my pelvic area. Also, I never said good-bye to my non-parent life, to my freedom and independence.*

☞ Relationship problems or interpersonal conflicts such as power struggles, hostility toward a partner, preference for another partner, distrust, poor communications, and stress can all emerge as pain during intercourse.

☞ Vaginismus—a cause of enormous proportion, and the main subject of this book.

Dyspareunia can be a source of great conflict and anxiety to the woman who suffers from it, causing marked distress and interpersonal difficulties. Although intercourse is possible, the accompanying pain has been associated with a more negative attitude toward sexuality, with more sexual function impairment, and with lower levels of sexual adjustment. The presence of pain with sexual intercourse is typically associated with low physical and emotional satisfaction, as well as decreased happiness. Unfortunately, many women are putting up with painful intercourse, depriving themselves of the healthy intimacy that should be the cornerstone of their relationship.

Treatment:

Dyspareunia can usually be treated once the causes have been identified. The clinician who takes the time to obtain a complete and careful medical and sexual evaluation can help resolve most of these problems. Medical and physical causes can typically be addressed by conventional medical care; functional causes require patient education as well as detailed understanding of her life in order to get to the root of the problem.

While physical incompatibility may remain a sad, unresolved situation, psychophysical causes can be cured through the body and the mind, integrating the two into a unified "whole"—the premise behind curing both vaginismus and dyspareunia, as discussed, in detail, in a later chapter.

CHAPTER EIGHT

What Causes Vaginismus?

*V*aginismus affects adolescent girls and women of all ages, all cultures, all religions, all socioeconomic and educational levels, singles, married and lesbian couples alike. And, contrary to common belief, sexual abuse is not the major cause of vaginismus, although many women who were sexually abused will present with vaginismus.

We received the following letter from a worried husband:

My wife and I have been married for almost two years and have had intimate relations for more than five, but in none of that time has she ever been able to have actual penetration either with my finger, penis, a tampon, or a gynecologic exam. Upon the initiation of sex, or any physical stimulation, my wife gets really nervous and tight, and there is no way that I can get inside her at all. She is very shy and doesn't want to go for help, but this issue is now causing strains in our marriage.

A common myth is that vaginismus is caused by a physical problem, such as vaginal polyps, infections, allergic reactions, or other dermatological concerns. We would like to dispel this myth because these are treatable problems that may be easily diagnosed by a careful examination, and resolved with pharmacological and/or natural agents and proper hygiene.

Another common myth has to do with the hymen being the cause of the problem—a devastating misunderstanding with severe complications, discussed at length in a later chapter, titled "Misconceptions about Curing Vaginismus."

So what is the cause of vaginismus?

The backdrop of this condition highlights a developmental difference between the sexes: Boys explore their genitals from an early age because they are external, visible, and involved in the basic function of urination. Consequently, when the boy has grown and becomes a man, he is usually quite clear on how his genitals look and react, how he fares versus other males in shape and size, and which way he likes to be touched sexually.

Conversely, the female's genitals are internal, invisible, inexperienced, not usually involved in body exploration, and their function carries a notion of mystery—an "unknown" that may be too scary to some female adolescents and women, a common problem of vaginismus. Of course, the individual's character and emotional makeup will also play a part in determining whether she will develop vaginismus, or whether she will be able to explore her body and emotions in a secure, healthy manner that is free of fear of the unknown.

Any traumatic experience, especially to the genital area, can have an adverse effect on the body and the mind, and can bring about vaginismus as well.

Consider the following Internet inquiry that we received:

In a couple of months, I am going to be married. My fiancé and I are both virgins. I'm very afraid of the pain that sex may cause. A couple of years ago, I had an internal ultrasound done to look at some cysts. My hymen was ripped in the process. It was painful. This situation has caused me to worry about the pain that I might experience. It is to the point that I am not sure that I want to have sex at all. I know that sounds stupid because I know that I have experienced far worse pain than that. What can I do about this? Should I talk to someone about this?

An important aspect of vaginismus, one that has not yet been given due recognition and which carries a tremendous impact, is that of being the *receiver* of penetration. In other words, being "done to." Anytime we mention this notion to our patients, there is an audible, visible sigh of relief from them, relaying the message: "Finally, someone really understands it!"

Unlike the man who is the do-er, the female is the one to be entered, a fact that carries a tremendous emotional impact associated with lack of control and with being choice-less, even if the man is understanding and non-forceful, and if the act is consensual.

This same emotional impact may spill into nonsexual penetrations such as undergoing a pelvic exam, where the physician is given permission to enter the woman's body, yet is being met with her body-mind reluctance to accept the penetration.

As noted earlier, vaginismus comes in different combinations, according to the particular emotional makeup and the particular causes that are individual to that woman. Our extensive work with vaginismus has provided us with a comprehensive list of factors that may cause this complicated condition. Some may be obvious causes; others may be hidden deep in one's emotional vault and will need exploration in order to bring them to the surface. Every woman will have her own combination of causes for her vaginismus:

 🍒 **Fear of the body and its functions, fear of the "unknown."** So many women do not know the location and/or composition of their genitals in general, and the vagina in particular. Common fears or concerns include where is the vagina? The vagina is endless; It is continuous throughout the body; Things will get lost inside; I don't have a hole; What if he will try to enter the wrong hole? I don't know what intercourse is all about; I can't even fit a tampon in; I should not tamper with my body; Will I ruin my body? Will things get stuck inside? Will I bleed? I cannot bear to look at blood, etc. We have met many women who would not even allow their partners to touch their genitals except over underwear.

The following testimonial about body apprehension was written by Tracy Morgan:

I'm a single, thirty-nine-year-old woman who had avoided romantic relationships all through my thirties because of my inability to consummate a sexual relationship successfully. It had just grown too embarrassing to admit to a man, and I had no idea it was a problem that others also had. Growing up was perfectly normal for me, and I was a little sheltered, maybe, but I learned about sex in my preteen years and had a good understanding about it. Starting in my childhood, my problem seemed to just be a general squeamishness about anything physically entering my body; I was perfectly comfortable, and happy with external (clitoral) stimulation. Also, I was always a person who was tense about any new physical sensations that were uncomfortable, or my body being out of control in any way, such as having a certain illness I'd never had before. My belief is that being that tense significantly increases the discomfort or pain of whatever you are going through. It's not that you're being overly childish, but that your fear is truly making the sensation worse, and yet you can't seem to forcibly relax. So the cycle keeps repeating itself. The same happened with vaginismus. My experiences with gynecologists were dreadful as they insisted I "relax" so they could examine me, and I honestly tried, but just could not change whatever it was that I was doing. As an adult, I lived in fear that I'd get ovarian cancer and it wouldn't be diagnosed, since I couldn't be examined. I found the gynecological community in general to be incredibly insensitive (and non-educating) about this issue. Tampon usage as a teenager was not possible—and I tried off and on many times over the years to use them, as I just couldn't understand why everyone else could do this. Through my twenties, intercourse was barely attempted, as it was "clear" to me that this just wasn't going to fit. I became convinced that I had some abnormality and was weirdly small.

When I heard about vaginismus on a news show, I thought this could be my problem, and contacted the featured specialists. Over a series of appointments totaling about eleven or twelve hours, we solved the problem. I'd had an intact hymen that truly was contributing to the painful sensation of trying to insert a tampon, in addition to my extreme tenseness, but I was completely normal and not weirdly small at all. Through gradual insertion of spacers in the office, with practice at home, I relaxed and got past the fear that caused the tenseness that caused the pain. We reversed the cycle. I started using tampons during the course of the treatment with no problem, and recently had my first successful gynecological appointment. No man in my life yet, but I finally have confidence that there won't be any intercourse problems and am really looking forward to it. I'm thrilled I still have the rest of my whole life to pursue a full sex life, and the bizarre possibility of actually living in silence with undiagnosed, serious female medical problems is, thankfully, a thing of the past.

❦ **Being worried about the fragility of the vagina** is typical of the vaginismus condition. Worries we regularly hear include "The vagina is delicate and cannot be touched, or poked or stretched; The vagina is protected from the outside world and should not be interrupted; The vagina is sterile and I cannot put anything in to dirty it up; My vagina cannot possibly fit a man's penis; My vagina is like an open wound; My fingernail/my partner's fingernail may damage my vagina if touched; Thrusting will damage my vagina."

The truth includes the following facts: The vagina is built to accept touch and penetration; It is not a sterile environment, just a clean area (have you ever heard of sterilizing a penis before intercourse?); It is approximately an index-finger long (10 cm), and ends at the cervix, which is the opening of the uterus (womb); and it stretches as necessary to accept a fully erect penis! Lastly, being of a petite body size does not imply having a small vagina! These explanations may indeed sound reassuring, but the woman who suffers from vaginismus will not be convinced until actual penetration is experienced firsthand, a need that is the foundation of our body-mind treatment approach, discussed in a later chapter.

🦋 **Fear of pain.** For the vaginismus sufferer, penetration is always associated with pain, whether it is realistic, based on prior experience, or just a perception without any prior experience to substantiate it. This anticipation is translated into an SNS reaction (Sympathetic Nervous System, as presented in an earlier chapter, "What Is Vaginismus?"), accompanied by the tightening of the pelvic floor musculature as a protective reaction against the pain. Structurally, this tightening reduces the diameter of the vagina, making penetration a painful physical struggle indeed.

Here is a testimonial from S.B., who was very frightened of the pain:

Admitting I had a problem and that I was the only one who could do something about it was the first step in conquering my vaginismus. With a personality that those closest to me label "Queen of Denial," I always assumed I would wake up one day and be fine, or I'd have sex and that would fix everything. Translation: I just wasn't dealing with the fact that my body would not accept penetration of any kind—not even a slender tampon. The truth was that after twenty-seven years, I knew this would never just fix itself. I also knew that I wasn't even close to having sex for the first time because I was petrified that the experience would be unbearably painful. I had my first gynecolog-

ical appointment at eighteen and never once had an internal exam. Since I wasn't sexually active, my doctor never pushed me to go through with the internal—she witnessed the excruciating pain I experienced each time she attempted to insert a speculum. It wasn't until I was twenty-seven that I heard the term vaginismus for the first time. By then, I had moved to a different city and had a new gynecologist. My new doctor mentioned the term, but we didn't really discuss it at length. I did a lot of thinking after that exam. Never once did I think I had a condition that actually had a name and that other women were unfortunately affected by as well. All these years I thought I was different, which upset me to the point that it was easier to just forget something was wrong. But something changed for me that day. I knew I was the only one who had the power to make myself better. I wanted my relationships to grow. I wanted to have a healthy sex life. I wanted marriage, and of course children. I wanted to be better. At that point, I sought help. The treatment process was intense both physically and emotionally—dealing with vaginismus affected me on both of those levels. I am a different person now. I may seem the same to people on the outside—I'm still the same out- going, friendly, fun-loving person I've always been. On the inside however, I have grown. Of course, I dealt with the physical aspect during treatment. But I also learned a great deal about myself and my per- sonality, and about the way I view life. Accepting that I had a problem and then making the decision to address it was the best gift I could ever give to myself.

🍒 **Past illness/surgery/medical procedures.**
Scary or painful events, especially if they happened in childhood, are common forces responsible for the reflexive fighting against being touched or entered. Additional complications may include the lack of understanding of what happened in the past, remembering being held down or forced to comply, memories of being alone and isolated during the frightening event, etc. It is important to note here that the past trauma does not have to have been limited to the genitalia in order to provoke such a reaction; the basic feelings of "done to" anywhere else in the body can cause the same reaction of feeling helpless, being "stuck," feeling pain, etc.

A wonderful illustration of this cause for vaginismus is the following case:

Esther scheduled an appointment in order to find out why intercourse with her boyfriend was so painful. She was a pretty, nineteen-year-old college student involved in her second long-term relationship. *My doctor says I have a small vaginal opening, which causes this problem. Actually, he wasn't even able to insert his tools for a full exam.* Esther was knowledgeable about her anatomy and needed very little relaxation in order to facilitate a physical examination. The findings revealed a vaginal opening adequate for sexual activities but dry and brittle vaginal walls with high susceptibility to chafing and pain upon touch, an unusual finding in such a young woman. There must have been other reasons and causes for the condition of the vagina and for the failed gynecological exam by her physician. Esther was eager to find answers to these questions, which turned out to be bothering her since her childhood. Her father, a strict Irishman, didn't get involved in her life. Her mother was physically abused by her own father (Esther's grandfather) as a disciplinary measure. Esther excused her mother's hitting her because *Her father was hitting her even when she and her sisters were older. Dad hits my brother too. This is where I got that stomach illness and my poor self-esteem.* At age fourteen and a high school student, Esther was diagnosed with irritable bowel syndrome, a chronic bowel illness. She was hospitalized many times during her high school years and was on steroid medications that nearly doubled her weight. Her skin developed stretch marks, she was reluctant to wear shorts, and had to give up on her dream to join the school's orchestra because of repeated absences. *I fought hard and was able to graduate high school. I hate bathing suits and how my body looks in them. I have legs and arms of a fifty-year-old woman. I felt apprehensive calling on mom for help but I had to . . . Especially when I got sick in the bathroom. I tried to tell my parents about how I feel but they took it the wrong way, like I'm lazy, bad, wrong, and they judged me negatively, as if I decided to get sick on purpose. They also blame my illness and me for costing them more money in school expenses than they had anticipated. They should have told me how proud they are of my achievements—taking extra credits and fighting hard to succeed. My parents always say things to make me feel worthless. I am surprised I haven't hit my mother yet. She has beaten and baited me so many times. They say they have the right to abuse and hurt, since children have no rights. When I was thirteen years old, I locked myself in the bathroom and drank rubbing alcohol; My parents found me and it was the only time my father hit me. . .* When we explored, in therapy, Esther's relationships with boyfriends, she told us the following: *The first time I had intercourse, it hurt, but I expected it. I believed it would go away after the next time, but it didn't. So I suffered in silence. I continue to do it because I love him and I wanted to feel close. But I have nobody to talk to about the hurts and pains. Also I feel bad about my own looks and body, and I get intimidated by all those gorgeous women around.*

🍒 **Religious inhibitions and taboos** play a crucial role in establishing vaginismus and are some of the leading causes for the condition.

The following short story is one of the most impressionable in our collection:

Having been raised in a Catholic home, I was sexually active in all ways except intercourse, which I saved for after the wedding. We flew to Switzerland for our honeymoon. Everything was so beautiful. We went to our room. It was intimate and romantic until I looked overhead and saw a picture of a Pope-like figure hanging overhead. That killed it all for me. I couldn't have intercourse. Two years later our marriage is still unconsummated.

In our experience, the particular religion is not the determining factor, but rather the religious guidelines regarding sex and sexuality for the female adolescent and the woman that are the source for inhibitions. We have worked with Christians of all denominations (including Catholics, Protestants, members of the Church of Jesus Christ of Latter-Day Saints [Mormons], etc.), Muslims, Jews, Hindus, and others—all blending together in a similar fashion when reflecting on their vaginismus problem and the effect of strict religious upbringing and religious expectations. The following testimonial was written by Valerie, who flew in to participate in a concentrated two-week program we offer to out-of-towners:

At nineteen, I never thought that on a trip to Spain I would find the man that I wanted to be with for the rest of my life, but it happened on a hot July night. Between the time we met and our wedding three years later, we tried to have intercourse numerous times but it never actually happened. I personally thought it was because of the fact that I wasn't married, and I had my parents voices in my mind chanting, "No sex until marriage." I had a very strict upbringing where sex was not mentioned at all, and I thought that anything relating to it and a woman's body was just something you shouldn't talk about. I can even remember when I first had my period, I was made to almost feel guilty about it. Besides the fact that I couldn't have intercourse, I was unable to insert a tampon or have a gyne-cological exam. I remember saying to myself I'd rather go to twenty dentist visits rather than going for the Pap smear. It terrified me so much I had to have the gynecologist prescribe Valium so I could relax a little before walking into her office. Well, when it didn't happen on our wedding night, it was very disappointing for my husband and me. You couldn't even imagine how guilty I felt. Deep down inside, I was hoping that I would eventually "get over it," but, of course, that didn't happen. After a few months of marriage, we were doing research on the Internet and we found out that there was a name for my problem. We were both so relieved. Now it was just a matter of fixing it. First I talked to my gynecologist. She gave me the impression that it was a mind thing and a psychologist could help me cure it. Well, three psychologists and one hypno-therapist later, I was back to square one. I was given relaxation tapes and breathing exercises to do at home, but nothing was working. At this point, I was very depressed and honestly don't know how I was able to juggle work full-time and still do pretty well at school with all the tremendous pressure on me. It got to a breaking point in June of this year. My husband and I had a long talk, and he made it clear that he didn't know if our marriage could last much longer and if things didn't look up, we might be facing ending it soon. I felt so guilty, and as much as I love him and loved him at the time, I almost wanted him to just leave because I just felt like such a burden and was making his life hell. In this situation, many men would not have lasted that long, so I considered myself very fortunate. That same evening I started surfing the Internet and came across the Women's Therapy Center's Website. I started reading about the clinic and the testimonials on it, and I said to myself, I have to give this a try because there was nothing left to lose at that point. I was so nervous leaving for New York because I didn't know what to expect and I went there by my-self (my husband wasn't able to meet me there until three days later). I still can't believe till this day that I started the process on a Tuesday and had inter-course the following Monday! I will never be able to thank them enough for saving my marriage at a time when I felt that there was no hope left. The only way I feel like I can repay them is by telling my story to others, and hopefully it will inspire someone with the problem to seek help, because there is a solution. It's a shame that most people are not aware of vaginismus, and it's not talked about. My husband and I are moving to Spain in a few months, and we plan on speaking out on the issue there because if one person knows about it, he or she can pass the word on to someone else.

🕉 **Cultural variations.** Intimate sexual relationships offer the partners an opportunity to explore their own individual sexuality, as well as communicate it to the other. Through this process, men and women develop their sexual experiences and preferences, likes and dislikes. Exposure to more than one such relationship, be it a one-hour attraction to the boy in class at age twelve, or a deep, involved emotional relationship as an adult, will validate one's own selection skills, sexual choices, and life's goals. However, such a liberal view is not shared by all cultures, nor are other sexuality issues, such as homosexuality, adultery, pornography, birth control, oral sex, body purification for sex, abortion, sex education, male and female genital circumcision, or polygamy. Cultural expectations have presented an ongoing conflict to women, especially in cultures that do not accept equality in the relationship. Such expectations include being sexually available for the man whenever he is interested; performing sexually for him regardless of the woman's sexual needs; getting pregnant as a proof of his manhood; minimizing her own sexual preferences; accepting the husband's philandering if the wife does not perform sexually in a satisfactory manner; accepting a divorce if the marriage is not consummated; disallowing use of birth control, etc. The resulting emotional and physical toll of these forces are devastating regardless of the woman's level of cultural acceptance, making vaginismus either an inevitable outcome of stress, or a retaliatory tool.

🍃 **Parental or peer misrepresentation of sex and sexuality** include statements such as sex is bad, sex is for the man only, sex always hurts, the man cares about himself only, or just pretend you like it and get it over with. Female adolescents who accept these statements without speaking up or without checking their validity, will often develop vaginismus as a way to avoid sex, which they have come to interpret as negative and painful.

🍃 **The inability to say *NO*** to an unwanted sexual situation causes the feeling of being forced, of being option-less, of the need for self-protection, alas vaginismus! Being pressured into having vaginal intercourse despite lack of interest leads to emotional disengagement and to vaginal friction and irritation due to inadequate lubrication. Women who suffer from vaginal dryness, and those who do not know how to manage dryness that may be caused by hormonal changes or taking certain medications, may become even more reluctant to engage in intercourse, developing vaginismus as a result of the conditioned struggle to decline or resist penetration.

🐞 **Childhood sexual abuse** is a devastating trauma with a life-long body-mind impact. It is an assault to the body and the mind, whether it happens once or twice, or whether it is an ongoing event in the child's life by one or more people. Sexual abuse invades the skin, the largest organ in the body; It overwhelms the immature mind that must now attempt to make sense of what is happening and of the rights and the wrongs; And it shatters the emotional being by imposing fear, intrusion, lack of safety, and helplessness. To cope with her fear, guilt, shame, and confusion about her body's reactions, the child will escape into the only component that she can manipulate, her mind, by blocking the bodily experiences, be they painful or pleasurable, forced or safe, often enlisting vaginismus as the protector. *Rape* is an equally devastating intrusion on one's personal space and safety but with an intellectual difference. Whereas childhood sexual abuse involves a youngster who does not yet understand her body and why it reacted the way it did, nor can appreciate the size of the intruder's genitals in true physical proportions (through the eyes of a grownup), rape victims have matured and understand their genitals and what sex is about (whether they are sexually experienced or not) and do not perceive the trauma as a measure of love or confusion by the intruder. However, vaginismus is still used by rape victims as a coping mechanism, and especially as a tool to reestablish trust and safety.

🖎 **Parental indulgence and over-protectiveness** are traumatic in limiting the child's ability to deal with life in a healthy, appropriate way: to face challenges, to overcome fears, and to face the unknown. Specifically, there will be voids in the following needed experiences: the need to explore the body and its functions, including accepting pain as an inevitable feature of life; the need to explore conflicts and the ability to develop constructive mechanisms for resolution; the need to experience mistakes and failures in order to learn from them and improve; the need to understand self, with one's own attributes and limitations; finally, the need to learn boundaries, responsibilities, and consequences. Children who are shielded from what their parents perceive as "the harshness of life" are often left helpless, with poor social and coping skills, and with poor self-esteem and limited self-definition.

The following true story is a classic example:

Jean was raised in an affluent home, surrounded by maids and an overly doting mother. She never had to carry a responsibility nor was she ever reprimanded; there were no boundaries to respect, no playing outdoors in fear of injury, no toys to put away—just a float through life. Jean never experienced having to make a decision. Food and watching television were the answer to any upsetting situation. And there was a socio-cultural pressure to look happy, successful, and to conform. Jean was quite bright and schooling came easy, but it was not so when she became an adult and had to deal with the REAL WORLD. She was afraid of making decisions as simple as buying clothes for herself. She became overwhelmed if she had to perform more than one chore per day, such as cleaning the apartment and going shopping, causing her to get "emotionally paralyzed" in front of the TV for hours, while eating until she became sick. Jean tried to keep it a secret from her husband, lying about why she couldn't do what needed to be done. She also developed vaginismus because she feared the pain she believed she would have during intercourse. Her three-year marriage was disintegrating. By the time she came to us, she and her husband had already separated.

🍒 **Failed penetration experiences** such as inability to insert a tampon or a painful first sexual or gynecologic experience will often leave a mark on the woman by way of fearing future penetrations in preventing recurrence of the same trauma. It is not unusual for us to meet women who feel that they are the only ones who cannot use a tampon because they couldn't put it in, or because they couldn't get it out. Another common experience is that of a first-time intercourse with a partner who was not experienced enough to realize that the woman is not lubricated, causing vaginal chafing, pain, infection, and a belief that penetration must be painful!

Here is what Jennifer, one of our "graduates," wrote about her life and vaginismus:

All my life, people have always thought that I had it "all together," that I was a stable and confident person. On the outside, that may have appeared to be true, but what my family and friends didn't know is that I really felt like I was a worthless human being. I had vaginismus, a sexual dysfunction that is rarely ever heard of. It is a medical problem that most doctors or health professionals do not want to learn or talk about. It is a condition that is traumatizing to most women who suffer with it. I was unable to have sex, to insert tampons or a finger, unable to complete a gynecological exam. I could never procreate, the only reason we are put on this earth; the most natural thing a woman could ever do. I kept asking God, "Why me?" "Why aren't there people out there who can help me, who can cure this mentally abusive condition?" At age nine, I started my period and developed as if I were in my late teens. In fourth grade, I was nearly five-foot-five, my bra size was a 32-B, and I should have been reading Are You There God? It's Me, Margaret. *I had high school and college boys asking me out, and I also had a very nervous father. My mother was not very helpful at this very emotional time. I recall her saying something like, "Oh great, this is all I need, a nine-year-old with her period." When we got home from the doctor's office, she gave me a pad. She told me to take my underwear down and I started screaming, "Don't put it up my butt, Mom!" I was too young to know where a pad was to go; I was too young to even have to deal with something like that! She took the pad away from me and placed it in the lining of my underwear. I was so confused; I thought that there was something wrong with me because of the way my Mom acted. None of my friends had their periods. I do not even think they knew what it was, either. I remember having accidents and bleeding on the chairs in class. My male teachers were not sympathetic and would not let me call home for a change of clothes. I remember walking around school with my coat wrapped around my waist to hide the stains all day. I think this situation was the beginning of my condition. Neither Mom nor anyone else ever explained what was going on with my body. I never really understood how my body worked until two weeks ago, at age twenty-six, and undergoing treatment for my vaginismus. When I was thirteen years old, I was going out with a guy who was fifteen and had already had sex. I remember he tried to insert a finger in me when I was dry and scared to death. It hurt so badly, I screamed, and he jumped away. He teased me after that, calling me "pinky slim" and "slender regular." From that point on, I associated fingers, or any kind of physical insertion into the vagina, with pain. There were also the emotional effects; the teasing really mentally scarred me.*

I reached high school and had a serious boyfriend for the first two years. He was sexually active and continuously tried to have intercourse with me. It was like a brick wall down there. Every time he would try, I would freeze up and hold my breath. He tried to insert a finger, and I would squirm and tighten my legs together. We eventually broke up for other reasons. I was too embarrassed to tell my parents, because I wasn't supposed to be doing that yet. So the years went on, boyfriend after boyfriend, with the same result. I was a very social child, I liked to party and have fun. All of my friends just assumed that I was sexually active. I tried to tell them that I was a virgin, but they still didn't believe me. When I got to college, I again had a serious boyfriend who had been sexually active for several years. I remember going to a party, having a lot to drink, and going back to his place afterward. That night, we tried having sex, and again nothing happened. He started getting really forceful and basically tried to rape me. I was screaming very loud and his roommate came in and stopped him. I know that he was frustrated and intoxicated, but it was not an excuse. This was another traumatic experience that did not help my condition. That time, I did the breaking up. I was so frustrated. What was wrong with me? All of my friends were doing it. Good Lord! Even my younger sister was doing it! One day I attended one of my Psychology classes that was focused on sex. While the professor covered various sexual dysfunctions, vaginismus was mentioned only briefly. In his brief description, he described symptoms that were similar to what I had experienced. I asked my friend Dawn, a psychology major, if she had ever heard of vaginismus, and she said that she had. Together we researched it and concluded that I indeed had vaginismus. That still didn't help much, and we were not doctors, so now what? I went to the library, the bookstore, and online to research the condition. All that I could find was a brief definition of it and some symptoms, but no in-depth information. So life went on as usual, and vaginismus was still haunting me. I did not know where or who to turn to, so I tried to avoid getting into relationships for a while. My last year of college, I met the man whom I thought I was going to marry. I got scared because I knew I was going to have to tell him about my problem. I held off for a long time. I just explained to him that I wanted to wait until I was married. He was raised in a strict Catholic home, so he was very understanding. Here is an entry from my journal: "I told him about how I wanted to have sex, I think I am ready after twenty-one-and-a-half years. I need to work on my fears and phobias, I am going to the doctor on Thursday, maybe he will have some answers. I have diagnosed myself with vaginismus.

Marc has been so patient and understanding. I know I can count on his friendship, he will stand by me."

When I went to my family physician for a yearly physical, he asked me for my gynecological records. When I told him that I had never been to the gynecologist, he was surprised. I told him that I was not sexually active, so I didn't need to go. He then told me that I was wrong, that I could have cervical cancer and not know. I did not mention anything to him about my self-diagnosis. I scheduled an appointment with a gynecologist at school. I was so nervous, I felt nauseous. She tried to touch me with her fingers and I freaked out! I closed my legs and would not let her open them. I finally relaxed a bit. She tried to insert the speculum, and I passed out cold. When I came to, she explained to me that I probably had hymenal tissue intact and that I would need a hymenectomy to remove the tough tissue. She said that this was very common and not to worry. I was so frightened by the thought of that. I called my boyfriend from a pay phone crying. My boyfriend wanted me to get a second opinion. I talked to a psychologist at school about the problem. He referred me to a psychotherapist/sex therapist that deals with sexual dysfunction. To show how vaginismus negatively affects young women, here is an insert from my journal: "We have not messed around for over two weeks. I wonder if he feels different about me since we found out I need surgery on my hymen in order to have sex? Or, maybe he doesn't find me attractive or sexy anymore. I do not know what to do! I am *really scared about the surgery. I hope I will be able to have a normal sex life—it is very important to me, and my confidence in womanhood. I will never get married if I cannot have sex or kids. No one will ever want me, I will be worthless!"*

My first visit with the psychotherapist went well. Finally, someone who knows what vaginismus is and how to treat it! After the second appointment, it seemed like all she was concerned about was why I had it and not how I could be cured. Eventually, she gave me a couple of dilators to take home and try to insert with K-Y Jelly. She instructed me to put it in, leave it in for five minutes, and take it out. How did she expect me to insert these things when I couldn't even use a tampon? I took them home with an open mind. I could not even get the smallest one in. I didn't even know where the hole was. I got a mirror, but still couldn't do it. When I went back, she told me to have a bath, a couple of glasses of wine, and if that didn't work, try taking a Xanax [medication for anxiety]. *I did all of these and was finally able to insert the first two sizes. It took me about thirty minutes to insert each one, but I did it! My boyfriend and I tried to have sex afterward, but I still froze up, and the wall was back. I quit seeing the therapist when my boyfriend and I broke up after four years. It did not have anything to do with the sex. Looking back, maybe it did? Another insert from my journal: "I am still working on the sex thing—I don't know what to do anymore. It bothers me constantly and I do not know how much longer Marc wants to wait.*

What's wrong with me? I'm always wondering who he has had sex with; I guess I just want to compare something or myself? Maybe I am just curious? This is one of the biggest problems I am facing right now. Why, God? Help me have a normal life!"

I finally had time for me; I started searching the Internet for answers to my vaginismus. In 1999, I discovered a Website called Women's Therapy Center. *I read the entire site while crying, shaking, and feeling dizzy. I could not believe what I was reading! There were other women just like me that were being cured! I was so excited, the next day I e-mailed them with my story. Then I chickened out. Shortly after, I met the man who is now my husband. We fell in love very quickly; we were engaged after seven months of dating. There was tremendous pressure to have sex. He proposed to me in the river where I was teaching him how to fly fish. He was on one knee in the water holding the ring that was attached to his fly line. When he asked me to marry him, I fainted, fell, and broke my favorite polarized sunglasses! I think I fainted because I knew that if I got married, I would have to have sex! The fainting also occurred two other times before. I needed to go on birth control to regulate my menstrual cycle to avoid it on my wedding day. I was already very nervous because I passed out the last time at the doctor's office, but that day I felt even more anxiety. The doctor was able to insert the speculum, but as soon as she started to touch the cervix, I started to faint. I scared her so much that she had the oxygen mask on me. She said that she thought she was going to lose me! She explained that sometimes when a cervix is touched for the first time, it could cause a shock to the system. She probably shouldn't have told me that, because then I had a fear of anything touching my cervix. I didn't want to ever pass out again, so I avoided going to the gynecologist. Another incident occurred at my husband's home before we were married. We tried having sex and I fainted. He thought that I was going to die. My eyes rolled back into my head, I lost all of my color, and he called 911. All of these negative situations were really taking a toll on me; I was in desperate need for help. I did everything I could to please my fiancé, even misleading him to believe we were having sex when we were actually having anal intercourse. I frantically tried to find another therapist in my geographical area. I located a psychotherapist who claimed to be the only person who could cure vaginismus in the area. She talked about all of these couples that she helped, and I thought that she was the answer. The first couple of sessions she told me that I was sexually abused. She told me to think back to my childhood, to ask my mother and my family if my dad ever abused me, or any cousins, uncle, or other family members. She wanted me to ask my mother about my swim coach; she said that maybe he was touching me while teaching me new strokes. After leaving her office, I felt sick to my stomach. "How could my father ever do such a thing to me." It was emotional abuse. The next time I saw my father, I was scared of him. I kept thinking about what the therapist said. I stayed the night at his house and was scared that he was going to walk in on me while I was changing. I was paranoid that he was looking at me in a sexual way. It was terrible!! I kept pestering my mother to think back to my childhood and recall anything strange about my father and me. That was my last visit to that doctor.*

I started having panic attacks at night, having bad dreams and thoughts about my body. The power of suggestion can have very negative effects, especially on those who are desperately seeking answers regarding a condition that is killing them inside. I really hope that this will not happen to another woman with vaginismus. I was so busy planning the wedding, and my fiancé was happy with the kind of sex we were having, so I repressed my dysfunction again. It was our wedding night and we ended up having "our kind of sex," and it continued throughout the honeymoon. Children are very important to my husband, and the pressure was starting to get worse. All of his friends were having babies, and I still could not even have intercourse! I began to panic; I knew I needed to call the Women's Therapy Center and make an appointment. I had better insurance, and some extra money saved, so there was no excuse this time. The hardest thing was telling my wonderful husband that I had betrayed him. He took it really hard, and we started having some problems. I reassured him that this therapy would work, that Women's Therapy Center was my last hope.

I talked to a couple that went through the "Out-of-Towner's" program. They had been cured! They definitely gave me hope. My husband was still skeptical, but he really didn't realize how long I had been researching vaginismus, and how few people treat it. I had a two-month wait, and I grew more and more anxious every day. So many feelings went through my mind and body. I had to open up and tell my parents, his parents, and my friends. I actually felt better, and everyone was very understanding. I wanted them to understand what exactly it is, and how prevalent it is. I wanted more people to be aware of it, so if they knew someone who had similar symptoms, they could help them. When I arrived, I was shaking a bit. I saw another woman, from Turkey, come out of the office. She had a big smile on her face; I could tell she was cured! I listened to her story, which sounded so familiar. If she did it, I could do it! I think I progressed quickly because I was willing to work hard, and I had faith and trust in the process. Everyone's case is different, and it may take more or maybe less time to be cured, but it will work. I never thought that I would be able to have sex with my husband, or go to the gynecologist without passing out. Guess what, I thought wrongly! I finally have a normal life! It feels so good to know that I am not crazy, and that my body functions properly. A lot of weight has definitely been lifted off of my chest and my mind.

❧ **Fear of pregnancy** has led many women into developing vaginismus as the ultimate method of birth control and as a way of saying *NO* to starting a family, to abandoning careers, etc. At times, vaginismus will develop after childbirth as a coping mechanism with the new demands on the family life, or as resentment toward being "stuck" with the new responsibility (the baby).

☞ **Fear of infection** is often associated with vaginal penetration, a myth that is in need of dispelling. The genitals in general and the vaginal canal in particular are not sterile environments, and are capable of accepting clean, physical contact. However, irritations and infections do occur, mostly as a result of excessive friction such as intercourse inside a dry vagina (very common in adolescents), or upon contact with an infected partner, including cold sores that may be transmitted to the genitals through oral sex. Basic hygiene and sex education should be applied as prevention, instead of enlisting vaginismus to be the safety barrier.

☞ **Social pressure** to be sexually successful often causes enough inhibition within some women so as to shy away from even trying to be sexual. The media tends to enhance this pressure by glorifying certain looks and by defining which sexual activities are the "norm." We will often hear from our patients and from male partners about how they developed their sexual expectations based on what they saw in the movies or on television. Unfortunately, reality is not what the media presents. Not all men and women look like movie stars. Relationships are not perfect. Vaginal intercourse does not usually last thirty minutes or longer. Women are not usually aroused to orgasm by vaginal penetrations only. And happiness does not mean a specific frequency of sexual encounters in a given time. Yet, the power of the media is enormous, and most people cannot distinguish reality from fantasy, falling into believing that the media is correct and "What I have at home is insufficient." Men will then tend to expect more sexual interaction, while women will unconsciously avoid sexual pressure by way of vaginismus as an easier coping tool than confronting emotional inadequacy, image misfit, and social misconceptions.

🍒 **Fear of relationships and of intimacy** may be managed by developing vaginismus, having realized that sexuality, and vaginal penetrations, are inevitable components of intimate relationships. In other words, women may rationalize their fears and inadequacies regarding relationships by assuming vaginismus, and by believing that they are not sexually worthy of a partner.

In this scenario, vaginismus is viewed as a medical condition, but in reality it is a façade for emotional difficulties.

My name is Stefania. For years I didn't know what was wrong with me. Not one of the dozens of doctors that I visited had ever used the word vaginismus. I was never able to use a tampon or have a gynecological exam without anesthesia. I dated casually but always men that seemed to be emotionally unavailable, I found that it was easier to avoid sex if we only went out on a few dates. I would convince myself from time to time that I was not meant to have a partner in life. Everyone has a problem, and this was mine. But then things changed. I met Michael, a man who I couldn't possibly walk away from, and I fell in love. I no longer wanted to hide from my problem but rather challenge it. I thought that as we progressed as a couple, my anxiety would subside and sex would come naturally. But as months passed and there was no change, our relationship became more and more strained. Several of my closest friends and family knew of my struggle but had no real advice or help for such an unusual situation. I was working at a small design studio at the time and had become dear friends with one of my co-workers. She was there to see my daily transformation from completely overjoyed to distraught and sad. I opened up to her one day and explained, as best I could, what was happening. It's such a humiliating thing to tell someone, especially in our society where sex is so prevalent. I always felt like I was the only woman on the planet with this issue and everyone else was enjoying a normal sex life. She was compassionate and incredibly confident that I would

*get past it. More than anyone I had ever shared my
story with, she was determined to help me find an
answer. She suggested that I needed to do more
physical work on my own rather than just reading
books and talking about my problem every week
with a therapist. I knew she was right, but my
attempts at penetration of any kind brought me
pain and disappointment. I gave up, feeling overwhelmed and hopeless. Eventually, I stopped therapy
altogether, and Michael and I broke up just a week
later. I kept myself busy with my day-to-day
activities, anything at all, just as long as it didn't
remind me of my problem. Then one night, a few
weeks later, I came home and there was an envelope
in my mailbox. Inside was a note from my friend
that said, "I hope this info will make all the
difference in the world." I read, for the first time in
my life, about myself in someone else's words.
I called the Women's Therapy Center that week and
now only two-and-a-half months later, I'm cured.
I've found new confidence in myself and I feel like
the woman that was underneath this burden for so
many years has finally come to the surface.
Suffering from vaginismus was extremely lonely,
especially being in a relationship but lacking the
support I needed. My goal now is to feel good again
on my own terms and rid my mind of what someone else expects of me. This is so much easier to
overcome without the fear I once had hanging over
me. I can't imagine what I would have done
through all of this without my friends and family
to lean on. There's no way of knowing how many
more years I would have spent with my feelings of*

frustration and inadequacy had I not reached out. I'm proud that I had the courage to open up to the people who share my life. I'm forever thankful for my friend who sent me that letter, which turned out to be the answer to my prayers.

🍂 **Fear of loss of control** may easily present itself as vaginismus by virtue of the act of intercourse: The woman is being entered by another and is the receiver of the act. Some women may interpret this primal feeling as loss of control, causing them to develop vaginismus as their way to regain that control. Edith's story comes to mind in illustrating this point: She was about seven years old when she woke up one night and stumbled toward her parents' bedroom where she saw her mother lying passively on her back while her father was having intercourse with her. The image of resignation on her mother's face and the persistent thrusting of her father stayed imprinted in Edith's body and mind all the way to her own wedding night, preventing her from consummating her own marriage. When she sought our services two years later, Edith experienced panic attacks during the first few sessions, triggered by her having to lie on her back for the treatment, a memory of her mother being sexually overcome by her father. It took several more sessions until those devastating memories were resolved and she was well on her way to a cure, feeling comfortable and in control.

🐞 **Poor self-image** and feeling unattractive can easily lead to body inhibitions during sexual intimacy, when openness and freedom should be at their height. We often hear women tell us how they don't like to undress in front of their partners, or how they insist on complete darkness in the room when they are intimate, as if to hide their own bodies. Some women will ask us if their genitals look nice and normal, others will doubt their ability to function normally in a sexual context. The stress associated with these worries will often facilitate the development of vaginismus regardless of the comfort and reassurance that the partner may provide, as the following testimonial tells:

I was born and raised in Tokyo, Japan. My parents divorced when I was ten, and my mother disappeared from my life. Being abandoned by my own mother was a sudden thing, and very traumatic. My father raised my little sister and me, and despite the hardship back then, we have a very close, loving relationship. I have the utmost respect for my father. I never had a proper sex education, and didn't even know what happened when I got my first period at the age of twelve. I was always the tallest girl in class. I also knew what masturbation was at an early age. Around the same time I had two occasions where I was molested by strangers. I wasn't raped or hurt, but was touched in inappropriate places of my body. Even though my body was not yet mature, my mind was. I knew it was very wrong, but all I could do was not talk about it and just forget it. As a teenager, I thought I was an ugly, unattractive girl. I always thought I was fat and the thought of being intimate with a guy scared me. So even when I became popular at school at a later age and enjoyed the attention I was getting from boys, I never had a boyfriend. At the age of twenty, I came to the USA to attend college in Manhattan. From then until the age of twenty-seven, when I met my husband at work, I dated a few men but was not able to be intimate. I was very awkward and tried to avoid sex. There was one guy I dated for a little; I even became physically intimate with him for the first time. But it was very clear he just wanted to sleep with me—he even told me he didn't want a steady relationship. Not only was I not ready for inter-course because I was so scared, I also didn't think it was worth doing it with him, so I stopped see-ing him.

I was twenty-seven when I met my now-husband, at work. We clicked right away. We started dating soon after that, and he moved in with me. He was a very sweet, sincere person, and I knew from early on that I could trust him. When he told me he loved me, we cried. I loved him too. We knew without saying that we were meant for each other. I told him of my fear of intercourse and he under-stood. He told me we could take it slowly. We enjoyed sex without intercourse, but not being able to have that special connection with me through intercourse started to frustrate him more and more. It frustrated me too. I thought I was inadequate as a woman. I had very bad PMS every month. I got very depressed and cried a lot. I also had an acne problem, probably because of the stress I had from all this. But he told me that I was so beautiful inside and outside, no matter what. We got married two years later. We were very happy, but we still couldn't have intercourse. Every time the issue of sex came up, I became sad, angry, and depressed. Sometimes I became violent and threw things at him, or verbally abused him. I even threatened him I was going to kill myself, although I knew I didn't mean it. It seemed like I did everything to avoid having to face my problem. It was really emotionally painful.

🍒 **Physical causes.** Occasionally, there will be vaginismus situations that are due to unresolved injuries or other medical causes. These will be as devastating as any other case, and will affect the woman's life on all levels, especially if she is in a relationship where intercourse is a desired activity. Consider the following testimonial from one such former patient:

I am sixty-five years old. My husband and I have been married for almost forty-three years. We had a loving sexual relationship for most of those years. However, about fourteen years ago I had a hysterectomy, which completely changed my life. Sexual intercourse became more and more painful as time went on. Positions that used to give us much pleasure were too uncomfortable to contemplate. I began to lose interest in sex. Then started the rounds of doctor visits. One doctor said there was a lot of scar tissue that caused the pain. Therefore, just "go easy" and that should help. It didn't. Another doctor said the vaginal opening had to be stretched. He suggested inserting a tampon the first day, two the second day, etc. Just the thought of it made me uncomfortable. The last doctor I saw suggested I use estrogen. I was not happy with this solution for two reasons—I already used it before with no help, and I also developed pre-cancerous breast lumps. Of course, all this led to marital problems at home. My husband tried to be understanding, but I guess it was difficult for him to fully understand what I was feeling both emotionally and physically. I finally was put in touch with the Women's Therapy Center. It took two sessions with them to discover what the problem was (internal vaginal scarring) and how to get around it. My husband and I are happy but angry that it took so many years to solve a problem that was really easy to solve. We're trying now to regain some of the lost years and put aside the problems that were caused in our marriage. It will take some doing, but at least when we want to make love, we don't have to worry about a painful situation.

CHAPTER NINE

The Diagnosis and Symptoms of Vaginismus

When diagnosing an illness or a condition, healthcare professionals ask the patient to describe what bothers them, what sensations they feel that upset them and bring them for treatment—the symptoms of the problem. Often, a diagnosis will be made based on the presenting symptomology; at other times, additional tests are necessary in order to arrive at an accurate conclusion.

We believe that diagnosing vaginismus is quite simple. It requires identifying an inability or a great difficulty with at least one of **The Five Penetrations of Life** that were mentioned earlier in the book, namely finger, tampon, applicator, vaginal intercourse, and pelvic exam. It is like going through a check-off list and marking the penetrations: If one or more are problematic, the diagnosis can be made right then and there. In other words, the diagnosis must be made based on functional inabilities, and not on symptomology!

So why is vaginismus so underdiagnosed? Why are there so many women who cannot have all **Five Penetrations of Life**, yet they do not get an explanation from their healthcare providers as to their problem?

- Healthcare professionals do not tend to get involved in the patient's life and do not ask personal questions about the ability to have penetrations, and

- They do not understand vaginismus as being a psychophysical protective response to penetration, and

- They are not yet aware of our **Five Penetrations of Life** as being the diagnostic tool for vaginismus.

Instead, clinicians seem to focus on the symptomology that is associated with the condition, a focus that is sure to deter them from the right course of action.

- I tried to lose my virginity in high school but it was too painful and then, I tried again, a year later, with the same outcome.

- As she began to insert the speculum, I felt extreme pain and asked her to stop.

🍃 My wife's breathing was no longer gasping from our passion . . . it was ragged with pain and growing distress, and there were tears in her eyes.

🍃 Our wedding night was my first time, and when the night that had been envisioned as one of pleasure and fulfilled dreams became one of pain and despair, I felt alone and afraid. I continued having intercourse sporadically, causing fights with my husband and feigning illness to avoid it. The burning and pain led to tears and stressful arguments, as my self-esteem plummeted. I felt unwanted and alone. I thought that it was all in my head.

Generally speaking, pain—be it physical or emotional—is the prime reason for seeking medical intervention or psychotherapy; more so when it comes to vaginismus, where the pain is both physical and emotional.

Although vaginismus causes a variety of physical and emotional symptoms that every woman will experience in her own way, pain is the main symptom and the one shared by all sufferers regardless of the severity of their condition. Asked to describe their pain, vaginismus sufferers offer more specific details:

🍃 Sharp pains in the vagina.

🍃 Burning around opening and inside, like putting hot peppers on. . . .

🍃 Chafing in the vagina.

- 🐚 A sensation of pinching in the vagina.

- 🐚 Pressure deep in the vagina.

- 🐚 The sensation of a needle/pin sticking into the vagina.

- 🐚 The perception of a wall inside the vagina that blocks the way in, and that hurts when pressure is applied against it.

- 🐚 A "poky" feeling by the urethra.

- 🐚 Pains in the lower abdomen, at times radiating to the groin area.

- 🐚 Rectal pain, especially upon a bowel movement.

- 🐚 Chest pain, headaches, jaw pains, neck and back pain—the result of the fight-or-flight phenomenon, the panic and anxiety that come along.

Additional symptoms may include:

- 🐚 Urinary urgency and frequency, similar to a urinary tract infection.

- 🐚 Burning upon urination.

- 🐚 Sensation of tightness in the vagina.

- 🐚 Muscle soreness due to tightening of the thighs together.

- 🐚 Numbness of face or upper extremities because of muscle clenching in the scalp, face, and neck.

☞ Emotional anguish, depression, resignation, hopelessness.

☞ Fear of pain.

☞ Lack of sexual interest . . . Becoming asexual.

It is important to point out that laboratory tests for symptoms tend to come back negative because vaginismus in not an infectious condition, although the symptomology may be suggestive of a urinary tract infection, a yeast infection, or other medical problems. The commonly prescribed medications for emotional illness such as depression/anxiety/panic will not be of help either, because vaginismus is not an emotional disorder, but rather a reactionary phenomenon to penetration. And the bodily reactions that are caused by the Sympathetic Nervous System (SNS) and the fight-or-flight response do not usually necessitate medical intervention, but rather psychophysical intervention for diffusing the fear of penetration.

It is imperative to emphasize that the pain associated with vaginismus is not "in the woman's head." Rather, it is a real physical pain caused by one or several simple physiological mechanisms, all which are in need of an explanation for better understanding of the condition, and for reassuring the sufferer that nothing is wrong with her genitals. But, first, let us give you a "functional" explanation regarding the structure of the vagina so that the causes of pain will make sense:

The vagina is a tube, starting in the vestibule (between the inner lips), and ending at the cervix, which is the opening to the uterus. As was mentioned in an earlier chapter, the vagina is approximately an index finger in length (10 cm), and has the capacity to stretch as necessary. However, unlike the nostrils and the ear canals, the vagina does not stay open but is rather collapsed on its own—known medically as a "potential space." To best understand this concept, we liken the vagina to a one-size-fits-all tube sock that lies in a "closed" position; yet as soon as a foot is put through, lo and behold, there is room for it!

More about the sock: To ensure it stays up the leg, the sock has a cuff, which is a narrower band. The vagina has a cuff too, being the outer third, or the first third of the way in from the opening. This vaginal cuff is there because this area is formed by the bones of the pelvis from either side, the tailbone from the back, and the pubic bone from the front. Together, they create a bony parameter that is narrower than the inner two-thirds of the vagina.

The walls of the vagina are built to withstand **The Five Penetrations of Life:** inserting a finger, an applicator, and a tampon, having intercourse (penetration, thrusting, ejaculation), and undergoing a pelvic exam (speculum and finger insertion). To help ensure the health of the vaginal canal, it includes many organisms that live in harmony with each other, keeping infections at bay. This concept of "good bacteria" (lactobacilli) and "bad bacteria" (anaerobic bacteria) that cohabitate is also found in the intestines, and in both systems, the balance is sensitive to breakdowns through a diet rich in sugars, repeated use of antibiotics, dehydration (insufficient drinking), hormonal changes, poor hygiene, prolonged exposure to a moist and warm environment such as a wet bathing suit on a hot day, infrequent change of bloody sanitary pads during menstruation, excessive friction, certain spermicides, and allergies.

Putting it all together, the vagina is a potential space of approximately an index finger long; it has a narrower passageway at the beginning, and then it widens for the rest of the way in; and, the vaginal flora—its ecosystem—tries to maintain a balance in favor of the lactobacilli count as a protection against irritation and infection.

Now, back to the pain in vaginismus. The chief reason behind this symptomology and the one that is always present is the squeezing of the pelvic floor musculature during a fight-or-flight response. This tightening compresses the urethra against the pubic bone causing microscopic injuries to it—urethral contusions. The body sends a message to the brain alerting it to this injury; the brain deciphers it as pain, or the urge to urinate, or burning upon urination.

In our teaching, we alert treating clinicians to carefully differentiate between a true urinary tract infection (positive laboratory findings) and urethral contusions, which do not require traditional pharmacological intervention. In other words, prolonged or unnecessary administration of antibiotics will negatively alter the ecosystem of the vaginal flora, predisposing it to further breakdowns and to potentially ongoing urethral contusions.

Additional mechanical causes for the pain symptomology associated with vaginismus may include:

☞ Finding the opening—a common theme that repeats itself with most patients. Where is my vaginal opening? At what angle should I approach it? Often, attempts to penetrate will result in fumbling against either the urethra or the perineal body (the skin portion that separates the genitals from the anus), causing unavoidable pains.

We were both virgins without any sexual experience when we got married three years ago. I was in a lot of pain every time my husband tried to penetrate me. After six months of marriage, we went to a sex therapy clinic; we spent a lot of money there but they could not help us. I then found the Women's Therapy Center. They showed me how to lubricate the right way, and how to guide his penis into my vagina. We no longer have problems with intercourse.

❧ The pelvic floor muscle tightness reduces the available diameter of the vaginal canal and causes pain when penetration is attempted.

❧ The angle of glide inside the vagina is imperative—nature makes us follow the "topography" of the vagina for a painless, complete penetration. However, lack of experience may guide penetration in a wrong angle, "bumping" into the wall of the vagina, the urinary tube, or the rectal canal, causing pain and further anxiety.

❧ Penetration will cause painful tissue chafing if the vagina is dry because of insufficient lubrication during sexual stimulation and/or because of hormonal changes, or if intercourse lasts longer than the woman's ability to maintain sufficient lubrication.

❧ Body memories, or the flashbacks of past traumatic experiences, will stir up the genitals into reliving any pain that was associated with the trauma, be it physical or emotional. This type of pain symptomology is different from the others in that it is psychophysical in nature, and necessitates specialized intervention.

In summary, pain may be caused by urethral contusion, not finding the vaginal opening, pushing into a tight vagina, penetrating at wrong angles, attempting to penetrate a dry vagina, and as a flashback to past trauma. Overall, one's ability to face, understand, manage, and cope with the sensation of pain is a determining factor in the resolution of vaginismus.

We cannot overemphasize our fundamental premise: The pain in vaginismus should *not* be a deterrent to intervention, as it is a symptom of the mechanism associated with the condition, and not a warning sign of trouble.

The following excerpts were taken from Beth's diary:

James and I have been married for almost three years! It seems unbelievable because of how fast the time has gone. My husband has always treated me like gold. He is the love of my life. We have always felt like we had a special love between us. This emotional connection has made our marriage seem like a beautiful dream. I couldn't have asked for more from my spouse. It has been the intimate relationship in our marriage that has seemed like a nightmare.

We live in Lubbock, Texas, and are very active members of a Christian church, the Church of Jesus Christ of Latter Day Saints. We were raised in good families and have upheld the strong morals and values that were taught to us in church and in the home. This included the "Law of Chastity," which includes not only abstaining from intercourse until married, but also abstaining from pre-marital sexually stimulating behavior altogether. We obeyed this law completely. We felt the blessings of obedience to this law including the blessing of having a great "nonsexual" love for each other. We looked forward to being intimate as a married couple.

I looked forward to being intimate, but I did not look forward to having intercourse. I was terrified. I had bladder infections and bladder surgery as a preadolescent and I had kept horrible memories of the many catheters that I had and the several unsuccessful catheterization attempts. I couldn't imagine intercourse being anything different than the pain I felt in doctors' offices and hospitals. I went to my gynecologist before we got married, and he tried to help me overcome my fears. He gave me Demerol [pain medication] *and stretched my vagina with a dilator. It was painful, but I was relieved that I was now "fixed" and would have a beautiful honeymoon. He sent me home with the dilator and told me to insert it once a day until I got married. I couldn't do it! It was too painful for me. I had never inserted anything into my body, not even a tampon. I went back to my doctor a week before I got married and he stretched me again, but this time he did not give me any Demerol. The pain was so tremendous that I thought I would pass out. Again, he told me to go home and insert the dilator once a day. And again, I couldn't do it. Throughout our engagement, I kept hoping and praying that everything would just "work out" on our honeymoon. That somehow, we would be able to have intercourse.*

We were married in the Dallas, Texas LDS temple and had a beautiful reception. We went to a nice hotel that evening and were intimate, but we didn't have intercourse. I thought it was because I was nervous and we just thought we'd try again. We had a week-long honeymoon, and we didn't have intercourse once. We thought that this must be a normal adjustment for married couples and maybe it just takes time to have intercourse work. After four more weeks passed, I started to panic. Maybe there was something wrong with the way I was built? What if we never got it to work? What if this was all in my head? What if my husband thought that I was not having intercourse on purpose? What if we were never able to have kids? My husband kept telling me not to worry and to be patient.

But after a few months, all my fears seemed to become more valid by just realizing that we had not had intercourse yet. This was an incredibly sad and tense time for us. Our relationship seemed perfect, except for this underlying problem. And to make matters worse, we felt like we should start a family. We prayed constantly to have intercourse and to be able to have children. We waited for a miracle. During our wait, we started questioning the nature and reasons why a Heavenly Father would create man and woman to have intercourse. Perhaps we weren't supposed to enjoy intercourse together, maybe the pain I was feeling was a sacrifice needed to bring children into the world. I knew my beliefs were true, but I started to become spiritually confused because our lives did not pattern themselves after what I had been taught. I thought that intercourse was supposed to be beautiful and to be used, within the sacred bonds of marriage, to unite a husband and wife physically. But now I was wondering if intercourse was just a means for procreation that wasn't intended to bring joy or unity to a couple.

As we were praying for a miracle, we read fertility books and tried to find a way to help us have intercourse. We learned about our most fertile days for conception and planned a getaway so that we could get pregnant. A miracle did happen. As we were being intimate and trying to have intercourse, James was able to penetrate the opening of my vagina. We both looked at each other in disbelief, and then I panicked. It was such a different feeling than I was used to. The panicking caused more pain for me. I told James to "Hurry up and do your thing!" I just wanted it to be over. He begged me to stop because he couldn't bear to hurt me, but I reminded him that we had prayed so hard to conceive and now he was finally in me and we were going to sacrifice the pain and get through this. I was determined that this would change our relationship forever. And so we made it through that night and we cried at the joy that we had finally had intercourse, although it was extremely painful for me. We believed our trials were over, since he was able to penetrate that evening. But the following days and weeks would prove otherwise. We still did not have intercourse after our getaway. Then why did that miracle night happen?

Two weeks and a few days later, I still hadn't started my period yet, and we took a home pregnancy test. It was positive, and we were so excited! I couldn't believe it! After eight months of turmoil, we were going to have a baby. We confirmed our pregnancy with a blood test and then told our parents the good news. That night as we were lying in bed, we talked and cried about what a wonderful miracle this was. I also confided to my husband that I was really nervous about how I would make it through the several gynecologist appointments needed for a pregnancy. I still wasn't having intercourse, and I had never had a pelvic exam. I really worried about how this baby was going to come out.

The next evening brought some unwanted symptoms of cramping. I talked to my mom who had cramping during her first pregnancy, and she and her first baby turned out fine. The following morning I started spotting. I was really becoming nervous about the pains and blood and called my doctor's office. They told me that some spotting can be okay and that I should try to rest all day. I rested all day and then as I got up to go to the bathroom, I started hemorrhaging. I knew that something was very wrong. It was after office hours and I talked to the doctor on call and he told me, "You are threatening to miscarry, it is very common, and there's nothing that you can do." That was it. I couldn't believe that my miracle was crumbling apart. Why did we have intercourse, which was a miracle within itself, and then miscarry? James and I were completely devastated. And the worst part was not knowing if we could ever make intercourse happen again.

Well, we didn't have intercourse again. And by the time our first anniversary rolled around, I knew that this was a more serious problem than I ever imagined.

We counseled with several doctors, sex therapists, gynecologist, and psychiatrists. There was only one person, a general practitioner who said he thought he knew what the problem might be, and he gave us an article on vaginismus. Finally, at least there was a name for what I was experiencing. Most of the medical professionals I approached after that didn't know what this diagnosis was, let alone how to help fix it. I felt so alone. I was constantly defending myself. And I felt that I had to defend the validity of the diagnosis of vaginismus too. I was told by one of my gynecologists "you don't want to get that (vaginismus)," and by my psychiatrist that "everyone can have sex." Was I making this up? It seemed like I was, since none of the medical professionals I talked to could validate that vaginismus existed.

These pressures, which lasted almost three years, seemed so overwhelming at times that I couldn't complete routine daily functions. I was so depressed. I had married someone whom I deeply loved, but I couldn't show him that in a physical way. I was mad at everyone. Every time I saw a pregnant woman, I would be so angry. I would think, "She can obviously have intercourse, why can't I?"

CHAPTER TEN

Coping with Vaginismus

*H*ow does one, whether single or in a relationship, homosexual or heterosexual, cope with the devastation of vaginismus—with the shame? The inadequacy? The sexual stigma? Being a failure? The fear that something is wrong with the body? The secrecy? Family pressure? The desire to start a family? The disappointment? The helplessness and hopelessness? The pain?

The need to feel normal within a body that functions as it is supposed to is the driving force behind coping with vaginismus. Feeling "normal" suggests being able to have any and all of **The Five Penetrations of Life** in a natural, comfortable way. Feeling "normal" also implies

147

being in control of life's choices such as managing menstrual flow, treating vaginal infections, consummating a relationship or a marriage, undergoing medical checkups, and starting a family. Emotionally, feeling "normal" means having the body and the mind work together, in harmony, toward fulfillment and happiness.

The sense of feeling "normal" may not always translate to specific words or detailed descriptions, as it is mostly a core feeling, a perception of *self* that is validated by the interaction with the environment. Feeling "normal" is a developing process that begins in infancy and continues throughout adulthood: Children develop through interaction with their environment, absorbing and processing information in order to develop body awareness, opinions, beliefs, preferences, and values. Nurturing parenting provides guidance, reassurance, love, trust, emotional balance, values and morals, and teaches conflict resolution. Life's experiences thus create a processing template through which all new input is filtered, enabling children to develop into adults who continue with self-assessment and validation as they interact with their surroundings: family, friends, colleagues, etc. Subsequently, an intimate relationship or a marriage provides the opportunity for further validation and development by the deliberate choice of a partner.

Sexuality is a life-long process of maturation, experience, and established preferences. It develops as an integral part of intimacy, of body and mind, not just sex. Sexuality is a culmination of harmony within the being, an outcome of integrating the emotional, behavioral, physical, and spiritual aspects of the self throughout life. Healthy sexuality is the ability to communicate through body and mind; to be vulnerable yet assertive; to be able to give and receive. Healthy sexuality is being self-assured, possessing sexual experience and preferences, being free of inhibitions, and never feeling "forced." Healthy sexuality is not about sexual experience but rather about a healthy sexual self!

The ideal combination of a loving companionship and sexual contact, such as in an intimate relationship or in a marriage, has long been viewed as conducive to good mental and physical health, and it is an essential goal for most people. Furthermore, for a relationship or a marriage to endure, a unified sense of satisfaction has to have developed. Long-term happy relationships or marriages have consistently been characterized not only by shared values, but also by a strong sense of shared activities, companionship, and strong communication skills.

Sexual intimacy is the ultimate level of self-expression and self-assurance within a relationship. It combines vulnerability with confidence, trust with trying the unknown, feeling and sharing feelings, and experiencing the utmost of body awareness while giving up control.

In no other aspect of an intimate relationship are the interrelated problems of the partners likely to be so clearly manifested as in their sexual interaction, and vaginismus is no exception: It places a heavy burden on the partnership and results in deep feelings of inadequacy, failure, estrangement, and disappointment. Both partners suffer, as does the relationship itself.

Vaginismus affects women who are single as well, posing a test of endurance when suffering from the condition. Although not having a partner removes immediate sexual pressures, the woman still needs to face the issue of engaging in a relationship altogether.

Common questions include:

🐚 Should I tell about my condition?

🐚 When should I tell?

🐚 Should I take the risk of being "dumped"
if I tell?

🐚 How long can I pretend to hold off on sexual
intimacy before my secret is exposed?

Conversely, the woman who is not in a relationship and the one who chooses to remain single still faces the same question of sexual adequacy, albeit within herself.

It is imperative to note that vaginismus is not just about sex—it raises other concerns that are common to all sufferers, be they single or in a relationship: the inability to use tampons, the inability to treat a vaginal infection, and the inability to undergo a gynecologic exam. Although these limitations may not seem as fundamentally upsetting as being sexually limited, the truth is to the contrary. Being the only one who cannot go swimming during her menstrual period places a social mark on the woman who would have liked to use tampons and forces her to either tell the truth or lie about why she is not participating. Not being able to treat a vaginal infection is a health concern, yet many sufferers are embarrassed to tell their doctors that they cannot insert the medicated applicator, in fear of being ridiculed or dismissed. Scheduling a visit to the gynecologist is a monumental hardship with tremendous anxiety in anticipation of the "penetration by speculum and finger." Furthermore, the possibility of suffering from a serious gynecological condition that cannot be examined and treated adds stress to the already-paralyzing state of panic.

In order to cope with the effect of vaginismus, women will employ a wide range of survival tools aimed at painting as normal a picture as possible, despite the devastation of the condition. As we are to discuss the comprehensive list of coping tools, the reader is reminded that not all vaginismus sufferers are the same: Some are not able to have *any* of **The Five Penetrations of Life,** while others are able to accept some of the penetrations, leading to quite a variation in the use of these coping mechanisms:

- **Rationalization:** This is an attempt in self-reasoning; to find an explanation that makes sense, such as "I must not be ready for intercourse"; "It will happen when my body is ready for it"; "It is genetic . . . my mother had a problem, too"; "I must not do it before I am married"; "The doctor told me that my hole is too small "; "I prefer using sanitary pads anyway"; "I am not sexually active, so I don't need to see a gynecologist"; or "I don't have a partner so the problem doesn't really affect my life." Naturally, these are not healthy excuses but rather a self-effort at minimizing the impact of the problem and disengaging from the need to address it.

- **Busyness** is a common coping tool aimed at avoiding life's difficulties. Busyness is keeping life so active as to disallow any opportunity for unwanted thoughts or actions to become available, such as the painful endeavor of

151

facing vaginismus. Typical styles include excessive volunteering, immersing oneself in endless higher education, becoming a workaholic, maintaining instability through constant relocation or traveling, etc. Yes, one can draw quite a bit of satisfaction from engaging in these activities, but they should be kept in balance, never allowed to become a compensation for other aspects of life that are being pushed aside.

🕸 **Avoiding**, the act of circumventing, of making sure not to come in contact, is another common coping tool—planning life so as to avoid any opportunity for encountering vaginismus, such as refusing to watch movies that include scenes with intimacy and sex; refusing to take birth control pills that were prescribed to regulate heavy periods because they are a daily reminder of vaginismus; avoiding dating and social opportunities to meet a potential partner. Other avoidance patterns include not going down the feminine hygiene aisle in stores so as to avoid seeing the tampons display, or using home remedies for genital irritation in order to avoid seeing the gynecologist. On the relationship level, means of avoidance might be starting a fight to avoid intimacy, pretending to be asleep when your partner comes to bed, or staying up very late until your partner is asleep.

🐝 **A compromised relationship** refers to the inadequacy and poor self-esteem that characterizes vaginismus and which will often prompt the woman to seek and accept partners and relationships that are less than desirable. One of our patients, a nurse, sought men who were paraplegic and could not have intercourse; other women dated or married passive men who would just go along without questioning the situation. Some women happily accept relationships with men who suffer from erectile dysfunction; others date much older men with a diminished sexual drive. Many are in relationships with men who are much below their expectations, but who accept the woman for who she is, regardless of penetration difficulties. Inasmuch as most women, heterosexual or homosexual, draw their sexual arousal and satisfaction from clitoral stimulation only, there may still be a want to experience vaginal penetration by finger, penis, or other suitable objects. Although vaginismus and sexual intimacy are most apparent in the heterosexual setting, it should not be overlooked in the context of lesbian relationships where penetration may be just as much a part of the sexual act, albeit with some modifications. Compromised relationships tend not to be maintained once the condition is cured and the women move on with their newly empowered lives.

❦ **Somatization** is the phenomenon of multiple and recurring physical complaints for which medical intervention is constantly being sought, yet for which a physical explanation cannot be found. In other words, here is a coping mechanism where the upset, angry mind sends the body to speak up for it in the hope that it will draw attention and bring explanations and resolutions to the unsolved problem. Somatization consumes one's life, preventing the experience of calmness, pleasure, safety, and healthy fulfillment of self. An integral component of somatization is the hyperactivity of the Sympathetic Nervous System (SNS) with its fight-or-flight reaction, which facilitates the establishment of a conditioned anxiety that will accompany the symptomology, adding to the sense of "being trapped and controlled by my condition." During the time of somatic experiences, the individual is convinced of her physical disorder, for which she would rather find a physical cure than face the reality of it being a psychophysical condition. This conflict will send the person on an endless search "for the right answer to my problem," eventually finding clinicians who prescribe medications or perform surgeries just to pacify the patient or because the clinician was not able to recognize the somatic presentation.

It is up to the treating clinician to be attuned to the troubled body-mind interpretation and to explore the symptomology while reassuring the patient of competency in understanding the condition. Somatization in vaginismus may include tactile (touch) hypersensitivity, chest pains, headaches, irritable bowel syndrome (IBS), eating disorders, rectal pains, sleep disorders, fibromyalgia, jaw pains, muscle pains anywhere in the body, etc. Somatization may also be used as a tool to avoid intimacy, such as the following quote from Tara's story:

With tears streaming down our faces, we lay crying the night of our wedding. I had always imagined going to the hotel, having a hot bubble bath together, and collecting our thoughts of the days' events. Then after enjoying a nice meal together, we would soon find ourselves falling in love all over again as we made love for the first time. Our fantasy was quickly destroyed. After having no luck in consummating our marriage on our honeymoon, we began to seek guidance from a doctor. When I told the gynecologist of our dilemma, she offered no resolution but that she had heard of this before. I didn't understand how, if she had truly seen this before, she didn't know how to treat it. I had never been able to have a pelvic examination before. Truthfully, no doctor ever tried. I always came up with an excuse not to have one. The first time I told them I wanted my husband to be the one to break my hymen. After that anytime I went to the doctor, was so frightened that it made it impossible for them to try. They could barely even keep me on the table, let alone do an examination. Every night I would make up some excuse not to try again, or I would pretend I was asleep when Mike would come to bed. I hated everything about our sexual life. I didn't want to make out, kiss, or do anything remotely sexual because I was afraid it would lead to "trying." I didn't like Mike to touch me any-where. I thought it tickled when he would fondle my breast. When he would try to put his hand any-where even near my pubic hair, I would cringe. To me, every touch, even the gentlest, was painful.

Separating from the relationship is an unfortunate outcome of the frustration that surrounds vaginismus. Everyone hopes that the partner will stand by, will cope with the limitations and will still "love me despite the lack of penetration." Indeed, most partners seem to show a strong commitment to the relationship, and separation is not usually an option, whether in a heterosexual or a homosexual relationship. However, this is not always the case. Some men leave because their sexual need for penetration cannot be compromised; others leave because they wish to father children the natural, biological way and are not willing to compromise. Some female partners leave because they feel that their intimacy is incomplete without penetration; some men claim that the lack of penetration reflects on their masculinity, suggesting a failure, and therefore, they must go on to be with women who can accept penetration. Many vaginismus sufferers encourage their partners to leave, feeling unworthy of their commitment and inadequate about themselves. Other vaginismus sufferers refuse to address the problem and allow the disintegration of the relationship, which they perceive as less painful than seeking treatment. The latter was the subject of the following e-mail we received from a frustrated husband, having met the husband and wife for a consultation three months earlier:

> *Thank you for the time that you made to meet with both of us. Well, our relationship died. It was not to do with the lack of sex. My wife became totally focused on herself and will not deal with her issues. This has affected me in a major way. She moved out. I must now go on with my life.*

🕉 **Substance abuse** moves coping mechanisms to a different level, where chemicals are used to numb the tormented mind, to lower emotional and physical defenses, to heighten self-esteem, to do what one cannot do when she is "clean." Is this truly coping or mere alteration of reality with little recollection of actual events?

🕉 **Depression, suffering in silence, and "going through the motions"** are emotional vehicles that signal resignation and the feelings of being helpless, hopeless and "stuck." These existences are the most desperate, with the sufferer having lost all emotional energy needed to cope, to continue searching for answers, to be able to find a positive in her life. It is like a dead soul within a living body.

🍒 **Compensated sexuality** is a complex coping mechanism that affects both partners in the relationship with devastating outcome. Compensated sexuality means being forced to circumvent the two penetrations that are directly related to sexual interaction: finger insertion and intercourse. This coping mechanism sets the stage for different means of dealing with the natural feelings of sexual desire, sexual stimulation, sexual intimacy, and starting a family by requiring modifications and adaptations, both physical and emotional.

🍒 **Outercourse** refers to sexual activities that do not involve penetration, such as manual stimulation, oral stimulation, masturbation, and anal sex (if the woman can have it, and only if both parties are in full agreementto do it). Looking from a non-vaginismus angle, these sexual activities are integral to sexual intimacy and are often viewed as variations from which to choose in addition to intercourse. However, when vaginismus is present, the option of "choosing" is substituted by "settling for what is available" because of the inability to have intercourse. Overall, it seems that not being able to have a finger inserted is not a major disappointment, just a reminder of the problem; however, the inability to have intercourse raises a magnitude of feelings. While the vaginismus sufferer struggles with feelings of inadequacy and of being a failure, the partner, whose coping is discussed in depth in the next chapter, struggles with failed expectations and with sexual frustrations. Some couples, though, are able to set aside the disappointments of vaginismus and keep a healthy sexual intimacy in all ways but intercourse. In other words, these couples are still clearly aware of the impact of vaginismus but are fighting hard to contain it as much as possible in order to feel close, intimate, and connected to each other. Unfortunately, there are many couples that cannot do the same and instead are avoiding intimacy as much as possible so as to escape the awful emotions that remind them of the problem. We often hear of relationships that have been reduced to being roommates, just friends, platonic, like brother and sister—reluctantly admitting to the presence of increased stress and estrangement in the relationship.

🐚 **The pressure to sexually please** the partner is an added source of stress to the woman who suffers from vaginismus. Comments like "I feel sorry for my partner," "I owe it (intercourse/sex) to my partner," or "I told my partner to just divorce me and find someone else to do it with" are quite common and highlight the sense of failure versus sexual expectations. This pressure is the reason behind the repeated attempts to have penetration at different times, in different positions, under different conditions, and for the eventual resignation and avoidance. James, a husband of a patient, wrote the following:

We went on our honeymoon full of hope that everything would turn out okay. Being physically intimate with each other was obviously something new to us and was not well understood. We did not consummate our marriage during this time. We just tried to be hopeful that the things that we were told about sex "taking time to perfect" would come true for us. As time went by, we returned to our undergraduate studies and work. The hopeful feelings from our honeymoon started to fade and tense feelings overcame us. We often found ourselves expressing frustration about not having sex in completely unrelated things. We would be short with each other or argue about trivial things. To have sex with each other became known as "trying." We would ask each other if we should "try tonight" to have sex. As time passed, the word "try" had less hope in it until finally there was no hope at all. Any penetration of Beth's vagina was painful for Beth and frustrating for me. The last thing I ever wanted to do was hurt her, especially during any moments of intimacy. I love her so much . . . I couldn't bear the thought of hurting her in any way. We had minimal penetration a few times. It usually was so painful that it didn't help the sex "progress" at all, and at times even made it worse. Sometimes we tried so hard to have sex that I thought we would go crazy from all the frustration. During these times I felt that perhaps Beth needed a break from trying so that she could relax. I tried to think of anything that would help us have sex, and help relieve our worries. I tried playing romantic music or surprising her with flowers.

☞ **Artificial insemination and adoption** are often selected when the couple wishes to start a family but intercourse is not available. Naturally, these options should not be taken lightly—each partner must sort out their feelings about not having a child the biological way, about staying a virgin yet being a parent, about having somebody else's child, and about facing questions from family and friends—difficult emotional situations that parallel the difficulty of overcoming vaginismus on one's own. James continued his journal with the following entry:

. . . *We were still only able to have minimal penetration a few times. Both of us were so frustrated, but we looked at these times of minimal penetration as a small glimmer of hope. We still wanted to have children as soon as possible. It seemed crazy to even think about kids when we couldn't even have sex, but we did. Beth got pregnant following one of those times. We were extremely excited. But this joy only lasted for a short time. Beth, just a few days after we found out she was pregnant, miscarried. Of course, this only made things worse for us. We felt like all the walls were caving in on us and our emotions were running on a high-speed roller coaster. Beth was constantly telling me that she did not want to be without a baby in this life and I was constantly reassuring her that we would have one. This desire was always overshadowed by the fact that we could not have sex. As time went by,*

*this longing evolved into a feeling of noth-
ingness about starting our family. We
began finding other things in life to do. We
chose to travel and start enjoying life instead of wallowing in our frustrating circumstances. It was a struggle to find pleasure in anything. At one point in time, I
came home to find a wedding shower that
Beth had organized for her sister-in-law.
Beth invited me to sit down as the event
was winding down. I found myself looking
around the room to see a few couples with
newborns and I thought to myself, "Oh yeah,
married people have babies." I spoke with
Beth about this and she was laughing because
she had similar thoughts. It was becoming
very apparent to me that I was becoming, or
had already become, numb to the topic of intercourse and children. We had lived without it in our lives for so long that our relationship could be characterized better as
two best friends living together.*

🐝 **Body shutdown** is a most powerful
coping tool for dealing with sexual inhibitions, with fear of penetration, with
the need for control, with poor body
image . . . with vaginismus. Body shutdown is a tentative state of existence
whereby the woman trains herself,
through her struggles with the condition, to deflect and resist physical and
sexual "want for nice" in order to

maintain a self-protective balance. When looking at body shutdown more closely, one can almost hear the woman telling her body not to be, not to feel: *My body says "yes" but my mind puts up a stop sign.* Body shutdown is a learned response, a conditioned pattern of reacting to vaginismus: *As soon as the pain is present, or as soon as the fear of penetration comes up, I stop. I do all I can to refrain from going on. I don't even try. It just couldn't work out. I then begin to feel guilty . . . and disappointed. I am convinced that my body failed me. I look at my partner and I see that he is disappointed in me.* Body shutdown can take other forms as well: keeping the mind busy with tasks to be done or with worries about this or that, interpreting vaginismus as diminished libido *because I doubt my feelings for my partner,* or hiding behind excuses such as being ticklish, being too busy, disliking men, or holding no regard for relationships. Body shutdown can easily turn into an automatic response, becoming familiar and quite comforting to the point that it pushes away the normal, biological response to sexual intimacy. Read the following quote from one of our patients who titled it, quite appropriately, "Body Shutdown":

The thoughts I would not allow myself to think, and the feelings I blocked, eventually combined to imprison me. The pressure of it exerted a force so powerful it created a monster of sorts, a dynamic over which I found I had little conscious power. I learned that this crisis had a name, body shutdown. I fell into the very detrimental habit of being a "sexual pretender" in many ways: I faked orgasm, I said "yes" when I meant "no," and I went as long as I could between sexual encounters. Not only was I reluctant at my partner's physical advances, I found myself behaving coldly and feeling tense. My unmistakable body language said "hands off" while verbally I would deny any apprehension. At the beginning I tried in vain to disguise my inhibitions, but as time went on it became impossible to hide. I felt like a freak. I was embarrassed, ashamed, and totally frustrated by my inability to express my love physically. On the rare occasions when I did try, nature would take over after a while and I would begin to enjoy the sensations. I would build steadily toward a climax, but just at the height of experience, I would perceive a shift in the whole thing. It was like a voice from deep within, screaming "NO!"

CHAPTER ELEVEN

The Impact on Partner

*D*uring the more than ten years that my wife and I have been together, we've experienced and experimented with a wide range of ways to pleasure each other sexually. Although my wife, early in our relationship, had some trepidation about oral sex and other intimacies, for the most part, she was curious enough to learn that she could allow herself to enjoy sexual pleasure.

Early in our relationship, while we were dating, she began to experience powerful physical satisfaction in the form of multiple orgasms and a high level of emotional satisfaction, with one exception: Intercourse was, in no uncertain terms, not going to occur. Since we were both raised as Catholics, premarital sex, which we defined as penetration, was off limits, and I, without much hesitation, agreed with my wife's feelings on this topic. We agreed to "do it all" once we were married.

For me, I was still receiving a high level of physical satisfaction without the pregnancy risks associated with intercourse. Of course, I expected that once we were married, intercourse would be part of our lives like every other married couple. This expectation was so far from the truth that today I have trouble believing and remembering the torture and frustration my wife and I went through for years.

During our honeymoon we immediately knew something was wrong, since intercourse didn't just happen as we expected. The time we spent together was fun, but something was missing. The problem didn't go away when we returned home; in fact, it became exacerbated. Seeing other couples who were enjoying intercourse was painful; family and friends teasing us about having children that we knew weren't coming was annoying; and constantly being bombarded with messages and stories about intercourse and children from the media and other sources during our daily lives was torturous.

Over those years of marriage we adapted but continued to be tortured. We would use what I call "Outercourse" to reach a new level of physical satisfaction. We continued to try new things, which added spark to the sexual portion of our marriage, but intercourse never entered our life.

I also realized that, over the years, I had become an enabler to my wife's condition, as she was experiencing a reverse addiction. Rather than wanting too much of something, she was avoiding something that she should have wanted and I was contributing to the problem. Although I couldn't cure vaginismus, I could have done more to find a diagnosis and help her find a cure.

It was extremely frustrating for me to see my wife suffering. I knew, and never doubted during our years together, that she wanted to be cured. This problem was not something that she was doing intentionally; it was simply out of her control and mine.

Once the person is in a relationship, vaginismus is no longer a solo experience. Although the partner does not feel the physical pain that comes with the condition, they are surely affected by all other aspects that involve the relationship, in addition to the impact on their own roles as a male and a partner.

Lesbian relationships should not feel excluded from this chapter. Although some of the content presents the impact of vaginismus on the heterosexual partner because of the difficulty with intercourse, the rest of the content shares the undeniable impact on the lesbian partner, in being a universal concern to any relationship, be it heterosexual or homosexual.

Sexual intimacy is a powerful vehicle for transmitting feelings between partners in intimate relationships. It integrates sex and sexuality with the special zone of intimacy that is unique to each relationship. This zone includes the couple's private feelings, actions, sexual experiences, and emotional connection, and acts as the barometer of the relationship, sensing positive and negative forces as they occur. Being able to develop a rich, satisfying private zone not only serves as the engine for the relationship, but also reaffirms the emotional and sexual maturity of the partners. Betraying the privacy of this zone is injurious to the relationship, and places a heavy toll on the trust and sense of closeness between the partners.

Upon meeting a prospective partner, the nervous system of each person will have initially guided the selection by way of physical attraction through the basic senses of sight, smell, touch, taste, and hearing; intellectual attraction, social and religious compatibility round up the process. As the relationship evolves, these attractions develop into integration and deep feelings toward each other, while the physical senses become imprinted for immediate recognition and positive feelings such as affection.

Conflicts, disagreements, or unfortunate outcome draw on the strength of each partner, and the relationship as a unit, to find a constructive way out of the adversity.

Each partner and each relationship will have developed its own style of sexual intimacy including preferences, fun, taboos, mutual consents, respect for choices, etc. Within this development is a sense of compromise—what do I feel comfortable giving up or modifying for the overall gains from the relationship?

The inability to engage in vaginal penetration presents an inevitable need for the partner to evaluate the relationship. This unfortunate circumstance is due to the breakdown within the sexual intimacy and the loss of natural hopes and expectations. Inasmuch as an understanding partner is an invaluable asset to coping with vaginismus (and certainly to the recovery process!), one cannot deny the struggling partner the options of self-protectiveness, self-examination, and decision making in a way that suits them best. Partners need to gather sufficient information about the condition in order to be able to reach safe grounds within themselves, whether it is to agree to compromise, or to break up if not willing to stay. Ideally, a partner will compromise until deciding otherwise. Our clinical experience has shown that straying from the relationship while putting the woman under pressure to be cured is most damaging and usually irrecoverable.

The following situations highlight partners' struggles with the condition:

🐚 Emotionally, partners may feel helpless and frustrated, not being able to perceive the woman's difficulties with such a natural act.

> *I will start off by saying that my wife and I waited until we were married to have sex. The first night after our wedding, we were so tired that we fell asleep in the hotel room. When we did try, it was very hard for my wife. We started off slow, with oral sex and gradually worked up to intercourse. Oral sex was never a problem for us, my wife felt comfortable with that. When it was time for intercourse—that was a different story. She began getting very nervous, even before we actually started. When we did start, it was tight and I could barely penetrate. She was in such pain that she would cry. By then, I would stop. It would hurt me to see her in pain during intercourse when it was supposed*

to be pleasurable. I was not a virgin when we married, so this was difficult for me as well. I thought this was normal at first, with her being a virgin, so I did not think there was any problem. Then this kept going on through the entire honeymoon. I was feeling frustrated now. This was not normal. Lovemaking would always end with her crying and with me being frustrated yet trying to comfort her.

🦐 Feeling rejected is another common complaint, stemming from males' fragile ego about sex, and their primal interpretation of the sexual act as a measure of emotional expression. This conflict brings to the surface a fundamental difference between the sexes: While men perceive the sexual act as a basic need, a tension diffuser, an expression of love and closeness, a personal validation, and a measure of success and sexual potency, women view it as a romantic, emotional connection, but only if and when they are not tired, stressed, preoccupied, upset with the partner, etc. In other words, to enjoy the sexual act, the woman needs to turn off her "thinking mode" and allow herself to be immersed in the physical sensations that follow. She has to feel emotionally close to her partner at that moment in order to "allow" sexual interest to take its course—she has to have her body and mind in total agreement of "doing it." Any fear or worry by the woman will sabotage the process and will turn it into a negative or a failed event. Obviously, the feeling of rejection that is experienced by the partner, be it rejection for outercourse or for reattempting intercourse, is the result of the woman's ongoing coping tool of doing all she can in avoidance of the dreaded activity. This feeling deepens the partner's crisis, leading to common concerns such as "She does not love me anymore," or "Is she having an affair?"

🍒 Feelings of sexual inadequacy are an inevitable outcome, especially if the partner is either a virgin or has only minimal sexual experience. The expectation to engage in what is known as a "wonderful experience" is quickly shot down by the reality of the situation, making the partner wonder "what am I doing wrong? Why can't I satisfy her?" The truth is that vaginismus is not about sexual skills but rather about the woman's fear of penetration itself. In other words, the sexual experience of the partner has no bearing on the possibility of penetration if the woman has vaginismus; regardless of the partner's experience, he or she cannot fix it for her.

🍒 Sexual void affects all male partners by virtue of their sexual orientation: However much outercourse may be satisfying, intercourse is still the cardinal way to sexual satisfaction and validation. The female partner, on the other hand, views penetration as a desired choice and as a proof of "being normal," but not as a needed component for sexual satisfaction.

🐝 The inability to either have a functional (hard) erection or to maintain a good erection is not strange to vaginismus. They are the partner's reaction to the emotional impact he experiences as a result of any or all of the following:

🐝 The pain and distress that the woman feels during sexual intimacy;

🐝 His fear of being the cause of the woman's pain;

🐝 The prolonged fumbling of his penis by the woman who does not know how to guide it into the vagina;

🐝 The woman's inability to lubricate because of her own worries about penetration, which in turn are being interpreted by the partner as a sign of his sexual incompetence or her lack of desire for him.

🐝 With the partner being the do-er, the one who attempts to enter, it is easy to see how the pain the woman is experiencing quickly translates to the partner's feeling as the perpetrator, causing apprehension, guilt, and reluctance to try it again. Even if the woman would beg the partner to do it in the hope that it will work "next time," most will decline or will stop at the faintest sign of pain, joining the woman in avoiding it altogether.

🐝 The social impact and peer pressure on the partner is monumental, ranging from assuming that "Sex is happening" to "How come you don't have kids yet?" The sense of inadequacy and the shame about having to live a lie take their toll quite clearly. The following stories come to mind, told to us by the husbands once their wives were cured. In the first, the husband was invited to a bachelor party for one of his friends, a common invitation for his age group. This time, he said, *I had a good time . . . I belonged . . . I no longer had to lie and pretend that I do it too.* The other story came from a husband who is a construction worker in a close-knit small town: *The guys kept talking about sexual fun . . . about getting their wives pregnant . . . And here I was, eight years into my marriage and still a virgin, lying through my teeth and beginning to worry that they know I am lying.* And this quote came from an executive who was also still a virgin after nearly ten years of marriage: *There was constant talk among the people in the office about who got married and who had a baby. Who cares? All I wanted to do was crawl into a room, close the door, and disappear!*

Modified parenthood is another area that is in need of reflection, soul searching, and emotional struggling. Since fathering a child the natural way is not possible, the partner must resolve within himself his position on adoption, artificial insemination, the loss of a primal need to procreate, staying or ending the relationship, how to present it to the family and the environment, and from where to obtain the emotional strength to share his feelings with the woman and, if needed, to act on them.

☙ Being forced to break up is common to some cultures and religions when the marriage cannot be consummated. It is mostly being viewed as the fault of the woman, but at times also as a sign of weakness and impotency of the man, who may be urged to find a "better woman." Vaginismus is a difficult enough condition to cope with without extraneous factors; it is quite unfortunate when the partner is forced to take an action that he is not at peace with personally.

☙ Religious restrictions add another dimension to the partner's coping by dictating sexual choices:

  ☙ Disallowing masturbation, taking away a major sexual option;
  ☙ Forbidding ejaculation outside of the vagina, a prohibition that eliminates modified intercourse with ejaculation by the genitals;
  ☙ Mandating having intercourse on a regular basis and at certain frequencies, putting tremendous pressure on both the sufferer and her partner.

☙ Sexual tension because of sexual frustration, hopelessness, and disappointment is an umbrella feeling common to all vaginismus sufferers and their partners. Despite the different sexual orientations between the sexes, both place high value on having a satisfying sexual intimacy. Voids lead to fighting, loss of conflict resolution, emotional crises, family tension, blaming, disengagement, and estrangement without the ability to be diffused within the intimate sexual zone. This is how Mike described his struggles:

Our intimacy as a newly married couple had long since left. Tara would sleep several hours a day on her days off and go to bed early just to avoid any chance of intimacy. Arguments between us seemed to grow more and more frequently and in most cases there wasn't even an issue except the bedroom issues of intimacy. I literally could not take much more. No, I didn't want a divorce or an annulment. I wanted to know whether I was going to live with this for the rest of my life or were we going to get through this. If we were not going to get through this, I needed to adjust my mindset for that and quit expecting consummation.

The struggles of vaginismus are difficult to hide. Both partners are attuned to coping mechanisms within the relationship and any uncertainty undermines the fragile balance of security. Additional struggles present themselves upon interacting with the environment that is not aware of the shameful secret and that expects life to flow in a normal pattern, such as parents and family, friends, and colleagues. Rationalization and excuses are excellent coping tools, best described in the following testimonial written by Eric:

I met Kim when I was eighteen and she was seventeen years old. It is now eleven years since we first met, more than four since we have been married. Last month we had sexual intercourse for the first time. Even to this day, none of my family members, or even my very closest friends have any idea of the ordeal I went through. Even if they did, there is no possible way that they could fully understand the situation.

I began dating Kim when I entered college. Being the typical teenage male, I began to push the issue of sex pretty early on in the relationship. To an extent, I was successful. However, whenever we got close to intercourse, I was shut down immediately. For a while, I accepted this as typical; after all, in consultation with my peer group, it was determined that some girls took a while before they were ready to have sex. However, the months dragged on, and turned into years. Finally, a confrontation took place about two years into the relationship. I was patient, but in my opinion, two years seemed like a really long time to wait for sex.

The discussion was candid. We had been together for a long time, seemed to be compatible, and planned on being together for a long time to come. I was essentially at my sexual peak, and although oral sex was great, I really wanted to take the relationship to another level. It all seemed like a reasonable request to me, and appeared to be well received. About a week later, we actually tried to have sex, and it did not go well at all. In fact, I came away believing that her vaginal opening was too small to accommodate penetration. It either wouldn't fit, or she just couldn't loosen up enough for it to happen. After trying for what must have been over an hour, we moved on to what was familiar to us. The whole experience left me feeling unbelievably frustrated. That was just about the last time we tried having sex for a long time.

About a year after that incident, Kim developed a yeast infection. Each time I would see her, it was clear that she was in excruciating pain. She had seen a doctor, who had recommended that she use an internal over-the-counter medication requiring that an applicator be inserted in the vagina. Months went by, and the infection did not go away. As it turned out, the gynecologist seemed to think that the applicator might not be getting inserted far enough into the vagina to cure the infection. Thus Kim was scheduled for a complete gynecological evaluation. The gynecologist seemed to think that the hymen might be preventing her from inserting the applicator. It dawned on me that this might be why we were not able to have sex, thus I was very optimistic to hear the results of the appointment.

When Kim came out of the gynecologist's office, she was practically in tears, and said that the doctor couldn't really make a clear diagnosis of the problem because Kim was unable to allow the examination to take place. In other words, she completely panicked to the point that the doctor could not physically perform the examination. Thus, the next step was to have Kim go in for an exam under anesthesia and a hymenectomy, if needed. The end result was that the gynecologist said that everything looked normal, and that she made a slight incision in the hymen to allow for easier insertion. The best thing that came out of the surgery was the determination that everything, physically, appeared to be normal. Intercourse was theoretically possible, something I had seriously questioned when we had tried to have intercourse a year earlier.

Soon after the visit to the gynecologist, the issue of sex came up again. This time I was presented with yet another excuse. As it turned out, Kim had suddenly become religious. She was now saying that she wanted to wait until marriage before we had intercourse.

Four years later, after dating for seven years, Kim and I got married. At the time, I really wasn't sure that we would have sex on our wedding night, but thought there was a pretty good chance of it. The night came and went, and the marriage was not consummated. In retrospect, I guess I was not really all that surprised.

In the next several weeks after the wedding, Kim's anxiety level seemed to be abnormally high. I had heard that this was not all that uncommon with newlyweds, so I was not overly alarmed. During this time period, the sex issue began to surface again, and for me, resentment started to build up. Something needed to happen.

Kim began seeing a psychologist, and shortly after that, we began couples therapy with that same psychologist. One theory that the psychologist had was that Kim had been sexually traumatized as a child, which was why she panicked about having intercourse now. This was something we had never heard before, and it seemed to make sense—even though Kim had no recollection of such an event. Soon after that diagnosis, the psychologist referred us to a sex therapist who promised we would be having sex eventually—maybe in six months, maybe in a year, but eventually. The idea of going to see a sex therapist was not a very appealing thought to me, but I went along with it because I did not know of any other options.

A month into the sex therapy, I didn't see it going anywhere. In fact, the sessions reaffirmed my initial thoughts—that it really wouldn't be of any help. The therapist would give us exercises to perform at home, and then expect a report the next week. Once we got home, nothing ever happened. Kim continued to see the therapist for six more months, and then realized that it wasn't going anywhere, and stopped.

Soon after seeing the sex therapist, Kim and I both started graduate school. The sex issue was more or less dropped until I was finished, and Kim was nearly finished with school. During Kim's final semester, we began talking about eventually having a family. Kim wanted to adopt because she was convinced that we would never be able to have children of our own. I, however, expressed the desire to first have children of our own, and then adopt. I really wanted to go through the experience that many of my friends were going through.

Feeling hopeless, Kim began to do extensive research on her condition. While browsing the Internet, she came across a couple of professionals on Long Island who specialize in the treatment of vaginismus. When Kim first told me she had found the answer to our biggest problem on the Internet, I was extremely skeptical. We had tried so many other things, and I wondered what these therapists knew that an entire battery of previous medical professionals could not treat effectively. Regardless, Kim was optimistic and wanted to find out more, thus I supported her through the process.

The initial two-hour meeting was enough to convince me that the therapists knew what they were talking about. They spoke with confidence, candidness, and told us exactly what they would do to address, and cure the problem. The difference between these professionals and the others we had seen was that they addressed the problem from a mind-body approach. In other words, they actually treat the physical side of the disorder as well the mental side.

Needless to say, Kim booked the two-weeks program while insisting that she would be the most difficult patient the clinicians had ever had (and I believed her), and that she would be lucky to be out of there in less than a month—forget two weeks.

To my amazement, Kim and I had intercourse for the first time after only a few days of treatment.

I could hardly believe it—after being together for so long, and never being able to have intercourse, it happened! In retrospect, it is truly astonishing to me that a couple could go so long without having intercourse. What astonishes me even more is how fast the situation was fixed, once treated properly.

CHAPTER TWELVE

Misconceptions about Treating Vaginismus

Hope Springs Eternal
by Ann

"*Fear gives a small thing a big shadow.*" That's a quote I read in a book I picked up at the Women's Therapy Center. It stuck with me because as I look back on my problem, I attribute part of it to fear and the other part to naiveté. I can't explain how or why I got to that point in my life, nor do I even care. The shadow is gone. Today I am a woman full of hope, promise, and endless possibilities despite the long ordeal I went through, and I no longer allow my *anxiety to control my life. I share this story for the sake of helping others.*

My story began over a decade ago when I went for an ordinary visit to a gynecologist. It's the thing girls my age did naturally. For me, it wasn't so natural. It became the worst experience in my life—one that traumatized me for several days at that time (and ten years beyond). Needless to say, I did not go back anytime soon.

When my husband and I were to be married, I thought it was important for me to use a form of contraception going forward since we would be sexually active and did not plan on having a family immediately. We had never tried intercourse before then for religious reasons. I made an appointment with a female gynecologist (because of my past gynecologic experience with a male) and refused any physical examination. My only purpose was to talk about contraception.

Not once on our wedding night or during our three-week honeymoon were we able to consummate our marriage. (So much for the contraceptive.) Surely I knew something was wrong. I thought maybe I didn't love him enough and because of that would not allow penetration. I froze every time-pushing him away from me. I even thought maybe we were trying to fit a square object into a round hole! Seriously, I thought maybe his penis was too large and did not fit.

Deep in the recesses of my mind, I remembered the story of a woman whose wedding I attended on a trip to Italy some time ago. Her marriage ended in divorce because she couldn't have sex with her husband. At the time, I remember thinking how unusual that was. Then I began to think we had something in common.

Over the years, we compensated in other ways for physical pleasure, but our sex life was almost non-existent. It wasn't even important. We focused on our careers intensely, which provided a convenient distraction, and we used our work as an excuse when people asked why we didn't have children yet. Out of shame and pride, we never once confided in anyone, so we had no support network. We felt alone, thinking this was a problem only we were experiencing, and we were too naive to know what to do about it.

After accomplishing our professional goals, settling into our dream home and finding financial security—now seven years married—we wanted to start a family. Still we were unable to do what comes naturally to most people. Even without full penetration, we tried to position ourselves so my husband's sperm had a chance to enter my vagina. It was a long shot, but we tried this ritually each month when I knew I was ovulating. At this point, all we cared about was getting pregnant. Having a normal sex life did not matter.

More time passed without results, and we went to another gynecologist—this time for a consultation only. Though embarrassed and humiliated, we described our problem. We were referred to a sex therapist, who finally named it vaginismus. I never knew it had a name until this point, so for this I was grateful. But for the entire year that we wasted, I am disappointed.

When you're desperate, you'll buy into anything. A recommendation from another professional was proof enough for me that this therapist would have the answer—so we took her word as gospel. We watched a video on the subject, which was a testimonial of a couple who was cured by repeating Kegel exercises and using spacers, objects that are inserted into the vagina to simulate intercourse. Our prescription was to manage our time more effectively, enhance the ambience in our bedroom to be more conducive to having sex, insert tampons regularly, and of course, do a series of Kegel exercises daily. I went through the motions, never whole-heartedly embracing these concepts. Even though I intuitively knew this wasn't the answer, I still went along. Nothing. A waste of money. A waste of time. Another year went by without a cure.

We bought sex books and videos. They only served to shut me down even more. We drank wine—even hard liquor to calm me. Nothing. The tension between my husband and I grew thick. Emotionally we were crushed.

After yet another gynecological failure—I literally crawled up the table by inching back each time there was contact—I was determined to make this my number-one priority. I was now approaching my thirty-seventh birthday and nine-year wedding anniversary. We wanted to have children and knew our time was limited. We were referred to another so-called expert, who took four weeks to call me back. I am thankful today that she did, because during that time I conducted my own research on vaginismus and came across the Website of the Women's Therapy Center— a dedicated resource for the treatment of this condition. By now I was willing to talk to anyone . . . try anything.

Since the vagina is not an external part of the female's body and is not touched regularly, most female adolescents or women will not be aware of any problems until they try to have any of **The Five Penetrations of Life:** finger, tampon, applicator with medication, intercourse, or gynecologic exam. Realizing she has a problem will send the woman scrambling for explanations, usually encountering insufficient guidance from mothers, female siblings, healthcare professionals, partners, etc., who may not only not know what to do, but also feel terribly threatened by the intimate nature of the problem.

Although most vaginismus sufferers believe that they are "the only one who has it," the condition has been a recognized phenomenon in the professional community, and a cure has been sought using various treatment approaches.

The basic premise behind current intervention is that gaining voluntary control over the pelvic floor muscles is the solution to the problem—the muscles will relax, the vagina will "open up," and penetration will be easy.

A second premise that widely circulates among clinicians is that vaginismus is a psychosomatic condition—bodily symptoms caused by mental or emotional disturbances—in other words, a problem "in the head."

Available treatment modalities are aimed at addressing either or both of these premises, which unfortunately are based on inaccurate understanding of the condition:

> The muscle portion that tightens up is involuntary and does not relax in response to conscious training exercises. vaginismus is about understanding that this protective reaction is reflexive and instantaneous, without cognitive control, and that the solution must address the fight-or-flight response.

🏵 The symptomology is not imagined, and
patients do not require psychiatric intervention. vaginismus is a deep-rooted fear of penetration—it is a panic reaction in the vagina.
It affects women across the board. It is real!

The following discussion presents common treatment
misconceptions and solutions that are being given to
women by others in the hope of curing their vaginismus.
This discussion is not presented in any order of importance or prevalence, just as a summation of common
practices. But first, we wish to mention that some of
these solutions may indeed be helpful in marginal cases
of vaginismus, when the woman needs just a bit of encouragement to overcome her reluctance to experience
penetration, and is then able to accept all **Five Penetrations
of Life** without any further difficulties. However, these
simple, marginal cases are far and few between. For the most
part, vaginismus is presented with intricate body-mind
conditioned negativity to penetration, which require comprehensive, multi-disciplinary intervention. Therefore, these
marginal cases should not become the standard of care nor
be generalized as the true characteristics of the condition.
Clinicians must come to grips with the fact that they do not
have an accurate assessment of the efficacy of their treatment when most patients will either be reluctant to admit
that they could not do the prescribed penetrative homework, or may never return for a follow-up appointment,
leaving a statistical void behind.

Verbal misconceptions are more prevalent than we
would have liked to believe, causing much more damage
than the individual who said them would ever want to

admit. In turn, they raise frustration, enforce dismissal of the problem, highlight discrimination against women, present a conflict of lifestyles, convey misinformation, and add to the emotional pressure. Typical examples are:

🐚 It is all in your head . . . Get over it!

🐚 You don't have a partner, so what is the problem?

🐚 Wait until you are married to address the problem.

🐚 Just do it!

🐚 Take a drink.

🐚 Smoke pot (drugs).

🐚 Relax!

🐚 Get some sexy underwear . . .

🐚 You don't love your husband enough . . .

Emotional misconceptions in psychotherapy, sex therapy, or any other psychological counseling, when the focus is on searching for trauma in the woman's past that may have caused the condition. Sadly, this treatment direction is based on the false premise that sexual abuse must have been the cause, an assumption that results in either alienating the patient, who resents such an assumption, or sending her home in search of a false past. In the same vein is enlisting marriage counseling as the solution for the problem, when in reality, most couples will be quite compatible except for the vaginismus component! Another ill-guided component of counseling is to make the patient feel better about living with vaginismus—an unrealistic compromise that reinforces the patient's anger and feeling of victimization. At times, though, psychotherapists will indeed give good advice and suggestions regarding penetration, including the use of dilators (more about it later on in this chapter), but since they cannot touch the patient for actual demonstration and practice, their good intentions tend to fail, because the patient is reluctant to try it on her own. In other words, emotional management of vaginismus, at best, provides support and explanations, but not a cure.

Spiritual misconceptions highlight an effort to enlist deep-rooted beliefs for the purpose of overcoming lack of knowledge or fear regarding sexual intimacy as a whole, and penetration in particular. As James writes, *In following our faith, we both prepared for our marriage by abstaining from sex. Our engagement was centered on building each other emotionally, spiritually, and socially. However, we both knew that once we were married, we would be able to enjoy that sweet intimacy that we had been looking forward to. The thought of this came with mixed emotions for both of us. As part of our engagement, we met with our church leaders and we were counseled by them that sexual intercourse was a process, and that we were to be patient. We were unaware that this patience would stretch over three years.*

Attempting to treat vaginismus through spirituality may be helpful in keeping alive the hope of finding a cure, in maintaining inner strength, and in encouraging the couple to find other means to nourish their relationship. However, spirituality cannot be a substitute for the proper intervention, a feeling shared by Mike: *We consulted with our premarital counselors about this problem, feeling it might be linked to some unresolved spiritual issue in our lives. They did some research on vaginismus through a couple of sources, and their initial instructions were to have a glass or two of wine to relax and then make an attempt. Well, you have to understand my wife. She hates the taste of alcohol. She tried it though for the sake of consummation, in vain. With still no luck, we consulted another gynecologist and our premarital counselor again. The pre-marital counselors told us that it was highly unlikely Tara had vaginismus—that only one percent of the population has it. They began to question Tara's desire to be married to me and after hours of her affirming that she did, sent us away for the week-end with instructions that intercourse had to happen for the church, the world, and the government to view us as a married couple. This destroyed Tara and me. What if we couldn't do it? That meant that the vows we took meant nothing. This signifi-cantly challenged my theological, philosophical, and moral views. The vows that I gave Tara were from my heart. To me this was no different than a cancer or other illness that may have affected Tara's ability to be intimate. To me the vows stood! Tara and I were in love and would stay together, vaginismus or no vaginismus. I have never seen Tara try so hard to complete any-thing in her life as she did that weekend. We tried every position, every kind of lubricant, and every room in our suite, for three days. We left that Sunday afternoon disheartened. We both knew something was wrong. To me it felt as though my penis was bouncing off a trampoline, and I could not get through. To Tara it was extremely painful even with the softest touch and plenty of warning and instruction.*

Physical approaches tend to make sense considering that they are aimed at addressing the functional outcome

of vaginismus, that of limited or impossible vaginal penetration. Unfortunately, their rationale is flawed and misleading to all but the marginal cases of vaginismus that
were discussed earlier in this chapter:

- ❦ "Kegel exercises" refer to the tightening of
  the voluntary portion of the pelvic floor muscles, specifically the Pubococcygeus muscle
  (PC). It was Dr. Arnold Kegel who, in 1948,
  championed the idea that these exercises
  improve the function and tone of a weak,
  stretched, or atrophic PC, hence the name
  for this approach. However, vaginismus is
  not about voluntary muscle control or about
  strengthening weak muscles, but rather about
  the involuntary muscle component of the
  pelvic floor, which is strong and tight because
  of its ongoing fight-or-flight activity. In other
  words, a good exercise is applied to the wrong
  muscle function.

- ❦ Biofeedback is doing Kegel exercises while a
  balloon-like sensor (perineometer) is placed
  in the vagina to register the strength of the
  PC muscle contraction. Biofeedback is a
  great modality for treating certain types of
  urinary incontinence (loss of control), weakness of the pelvic floor after childbirth, and
  other conditions of reduced muscle tone in
  the pelvic floor area, but not vaginismus.

- ❦ Electrical stimulation is still another variation
  of working on the pelvic floor muscles, this

time by way of delivering an electrical current that stimulates them to contract (tighten). This technique is quite useful when treating certain medical conditions, but not the type of muscle reaction that is present in vaginismus. To illustrate this misconception, here is a true story about vaginismus and the sensation of "tingling," which is perfectly normal during electrical stimulation: This professional attempted to treat vaginismus by placing electrical stimulation electrodes on the male penis and inside the female vagina, then instructed them to have intercourse while the current was on. It was claimed that they were able to have intercourse, albeit not feeling much more than the "buzz." We then inquired about subsequent attempts by the couple to have intercourse and about being able to move from a clinical experience to sexual intimacy (a cure!); sadly, all the clinician was able to say was, *Well, they did it once to consummate the relationship; it is okay if they never do it again,* a disturbing attitude from a professional whose mission is to help restore normalcy!

🎗 Hypnosis, a state that resembles sleep but is induced by a person whose suggestions are readily accepted by the subject, seems to be quite a common treatment modality for vaginismus. The premise behind this intervention is that since vaginismus is a psychological condition, once the woman understands that the problem lies within the unconscious and that she is

completely capable physically (was a gynecologic exam possible to substantiate this?),
then the acceptance of suggestion will lead
to a cure. Common suggestions during hypnosis include 1) Sex is as natural as breathing; 2) Sex is the act of procreation; 3) It is
acceptable to openly give yourself to someone you love and accept; 4) Any inappropriate behavior in your past was not your fault,
etc. The truth is that vaginismus makes a
woman *physically* incapable . . . Vaginismus
is not about disliking sex . . . Abuse is only
one of many causes for the condition . . .
And vaginismus in definitely not about not
loving the partner or not wanting to be intimate! Therefore, hypnosis may be a beneficial
therapeutic vehicle for some conditions, but
not for this one, where the woman needs to
undo her fear of penetration while she is
conscious and aware of bodily feelings in
order to be able to take it to the next level of
sexual intimacy. Furthermore, what about
using a tampon or going to the gynecologist?
This is what James wrote about their experience
regarding this issue:

*We were required to buy the tapes and he told
my wife to listen to them each day for at least
two hours. Upon completing the hypnosis, she was
supposed to begin her vaginal exercises, meaning
she was to do a series of Kegel exercises and to then
insert a plastic dilator. He promised instant results.*

Beth was eager to start, but her anticipation was quickly shattered. I received a phone call from her while I was at work. She said that the process had been a complete failure. Beth had nothing but utter fear in her voice. She was losing all hope and thought that we would never be able to have sex. Although I didn't want her to know, I was beginning to worry too. I had no way to fix our predicament. I called the therapist and told him that we were canceling all future appointments. He was surprised and asked why. I told him about the awful experience that Beth had. I was shocked and angry at his response. He said that Beth was just mentally running away. He arrogantly stated that he was certain that we would not get better and that in a year we would be back to visit him. I was so mad. I knew that the last thing Beth was doing was running away from her problems. She was constantly looking for help to cure vaginismus. She was trying everything, even when it seemed hopeless. The problem with this doctor, and the many others we saw, was that they told us that vaginismus was just a "relaxing" problem. They kept telling us that if Beth could relax, then we could have sex.

Relaxation techniques—a wonderful tool for stress management, be it audiotapes, visualization techniques, imagery, or any other vehicle that the person relates to on their way to reducing stress and regaining calmness. However, most vaginismus sufferers are quite calm except for when penetration is involved, in which case no relaxation will alter the mind's fear of the activity. Vaginismus is not about de-stressing, it is about the fight-or-flight response, which is way beyond relaxation exercises!

Here is Mike's experience with this approach:

> *With some reluctance, the doctor made arrangements for Tara to see a sex therapist who won our confidence, telling us that this is an easily treated problem. She told us that with some counseling and homework projects, she could be healed in three to four years. All Tara would need to do was introduce my finger or hers into her vagina each night for a few minutes and concentrate on relaxing. They practiced relaxation exercises day after day as Tara sat in the chair in her office with absolutely nothing causing her to be stressed. Each night was a different story however. Tara refused to use her own finger, telling me how grotesque it was. Each time I tried, it sent her to the roof in screams of pain with tears rolling down her soft, innocent face. I was so confused. I assumed I was doing what I was supposed to do. I didn't understand, though, how my sticking my finger in a hole that was scared to have anything in it was going to make it better. After a few sessions with absolutely no progress, Tara refused to go back.*

Dilators—the clinician's magical cure for vaginismus! This treatment concept makes sense only if one does not have a true understanding of the condition. An enlightened clinician will realize that it does not work. *The doctor finally told me what she thought was wrong. She had me read a section from her medical dictionary about vaginismus. I had never heard the term before, but the description fit me to a tee. Finally I knew why the exams were painful. She also told me to order, through the mail, a set of "dilators." I was supposed to practice with the set and return to see her in a few months. I received the dilator set in the mail. Upon opening it, I saw a plastic bag with large rubber cone-shaped objects. There was absolutely no way I would consider using these things. They scared the heck out of me. I never used a tampon, did not know about my own body. I was not about to start trying with these strange-looking things. The box went into the closet, not to be seen again.*

Some clinicians show the dilators to the women as they describe the treatment; others arrange for a mail order directly to the patient's house. Dilators come in different shapes, colors, and sizes; some doctors will suggest the use of tampons, or give syringes of various sizes to be used as dilators despite their unfriendly shape to the vagina (and to the mind). Instructions for use are basically the same regardless of the type of dilator given:

- 🍄 Gradual insertion;

- 🍄 One size at a time;

- 🍄 In the privacy of the woman's own home;

- 🍄 At her own pace.

Women are usually sent home to wait for the dilator set to arrive by mail and to practice on their own, without hands-on training at the clinician's office. At times, a gynecologist may demonstrate by inserting a finger or a tampon into a woman's vagina, then send her home to do it all on her own. Some clinicians give dilators to the patient while in their office and ask them to self-insert and ring a bell once they succeed. None sits down with the patient for ongoing, personalized guidance of penetration. These approaches are responsible for the following misconceptions about dilators' success:

- Those who suffer from vaginismus do not usually know their genitals, and the thought of having to "look and touch" is often overwhelming and impossible.

- Most vaginismus sufferers would not touch themselves for insertion because it scares them too much.

- They are so afraid of the penetration being painful that they cannot "do it to themselves."

- Vaginismus sufferers do not know where the vaginal opening is, how to insert, at what angle, how deep they can actually go, etc.

- They do not know how to properly lubricate to avoid unnecessary chafing and additional pain.

- By itself, self-insertion with dilators is impractical, in being far from resembling **The Five Penetrations of Life.**

- Myth: "Doing it in private" is helpful. Truth: Women who suffer from vaginismus need hands-on guidance and reassurance; they cannot do it on their own or they would not have had the condition in the first place!

- Working at their "own pace" is another ill-guided thought: The fight-or-flight response is not supportive of proper pacing—it either activates more stress, or it sends the woman into "avoidance."

🌸 Another fundamental flaw to dilators is the missing transition into sexual intimacy with another individual who will be doing the penetration. Even if the woman is able to use dilators, as in those marginal cases we mentioned earlier, and even if she had her partner participate in the insertion (an important step!), how does she move from that to the five penetrations?

🌸 The dilator sets are not measured to include realistic sizes of penises at full erection, they are not matching the partner's actual size (Yes, there are differences!), and the practice does not simulate actual intercourse or how to use a tampon or have a gynecologic exam. In other words, inasmuch as dilators are a sound concept for introducing penetration, they lack the necessary demonstration, guidance, realistic details, and applicability necessary to cure the condition. An example that stands out is of a patient who was given syringes of various sizes by her female gynecologist and sent home to practice penetration. Yes, she was able to do that but still could not have intercourse and consummate her marriage. When she consulted with us, we learned that she had no idea how to move from self-inserting the syringes to guiding her husband's penis into her vagina, not understanding why he poked into her genitals without finding his way in. This was a simple case to solve, yet illustrative of the need for applicable guidance with hands-on demonstration.

The following is from an Internet inquiry we received about an ideal situation of dilator success but failure to reach a cure: *We used the dilators and I learned to relax and got to the last one quite quickly. I was really pleased. But when it came to transferring to my husband, we soon realized that even the last dilator was way smaller in diameter, and we just couldn't bridge the gap. We told the sex therapist this, but it seemed like she wanted to make us go back over all the ground we'd covered. We'd done so much to help ourselves already, including some marital counseling; she couldn't see that we weren't starting from scratch. Since then, we have invested in a vibrator that we use as a dilator just because it's a realistic size. It makes you feel pretty scummy when you have to order from a sex catalogue to deal with a medical condition. I am able to insert it slowly, but still we can't seem to make the transition.*

Sex-oriented misconceptions center on sexual arousal, which is viewed as a necessary component to reaching a cure. Generally, intervention includes sex therapy to enhance sexual skills, relaxation techniques, and the use of dilators while employing sexual imagery or viewing pornographic tapes for sexual stimulation purposes. According to this approach, vaginismus is not a physical problem but rather psychological, and it is easily treated by way of teaching the vagina to have conscious control so that it will stay relaxed and accept penetration. The dilators' use is identical to what was discussed above. The transition from dilators to intercourse is done with the woman on top of the man for "assuming control," guiding his penis into her vagina as she is lowering herself down on him while doing Kegel exercises to maintain control of her PC muscle. Unfortunately, so many told us how this technique is unthinkable because they could not fathom giving themselves more pain by sliding down on the partner's erect penis. A common quote is, *I couldn't get anything inside me, so how was that going to work? The only control it gave me was to not do it at all.* Additionally, this approach blends vaginismus with sexual arousal and disregards the rest of the five penetrations.

The misconception here is linking penetration with sexual stimulation. The truth is that fear of penetration is in opposition to sexual arousal, one involving the Sympathetic Nervous System (SNS) while the other involving the Parasympathetic Nervous System—two opposing mechanisms! One rests when the other works, as they do not work at the same time.

Furthermore, vaginismus is not about sexual skills or sexual arousal. These feelings are far from the woman's mind at that time. All she is concerned with are the worries about pain and fear. Female sexuality is ruled by emotional state, and any worry a woman may experience will prevent sexual arousal from taking place. Therefore, proper treatment should enable the woman to first understand her body and be able to have penetrations before she shares herself, sexually, with herself or with another person.

The **medical misconceptions** stem from viewing vaginismus as a physical condition, a structural anomality, or simply a "head problem." With limited training in the understanding of this condition, physicians are pressed to be able to make an accurate diagnosis, give the patient sufficient explanations, and have knowledge of a specialist who treats the condition to make a referral . . . difficult tasks that falter regularly. Exceptions are those physicians who are attuned to their limitations and have taken steps to expand their knowledge and professional contacts, such as this gynecologist who sent us an e-mail saying, *I am an OBGYN with an interest in vaginismus. I have several new patients with this condition and would like to educate myself as much as possible with how to best treat them, so I would be interested in any information you could provide me.* Unfortunately, most physicians are not attuned to this problem and either dismiss it as a "head problem" or choose to ignore it until the woman brings it up to them. Two typical examples that come to mind are the physician who has known about his patient's vaginismus for several years but chose not to tell her until eight weeks prior to her wedding, and the physician who would not explain to her eighteen-year-old patient why she couldn't have a pelvic exam or use tampons, yet made light of it when the patient returned with results of her own medical research! Another distressing fact is that many physicians, especially males, are uncomfortable taking sexual history or inquiring about intimate matters such as penetrations, and prefer to treat the patient under the assumption that all is well. From the patient's point of view, she feels so embarrassed and ashamed about her vaginismus that she will not tend to bring up the topic either, but rather go on also pretending that all is fine. Here is what Beth wrote about such an experience:

> *We counseled with several doctors, sex therapists, gynecologists, and psychiatrists. There was only one person, a general practitioner who said he thought he knew what the problem might be, and he gave us an article on vaginismus. Finally, at least there was a name for what I was experiencing. Most of the medical professionals I approached after that didn't know what this diagnosis was, let alone how to help fix it. I felt so alone. I was constantly defending myself. And I felt that I had to defend the validity of the diagnosis of vaginismus too. I was told by one of my gynecologists, "You don't want to get that," and by my psychiatrist that "Everyone can have sex." Was I making this up? It seemed like I was, since none of the medical professionals I talked to could validate that vaginismus existed.*

The encouraging news is that some gynecologists have taken to employing nurses who meet with patients for in-depth assessments, including inquiries regarding relationships, abuse, and penetration difficulties. These nurses are able to alert the physicians to special needs, make referral to specialists, and provide the patient with the necessary initial emotional support. However, most physicians either believe that none of their patients have vaginismus, or tend to address the condition in one or more of the following ways:

🦋 Dismissal, as the following Internet inquiry illustrates: *I went to a doctor who was rude and arrogant and told me, "Don't be ridiculous. There is nothing wrong with you. You will get over it." I went back to him and he told me he thought I might have vaginismus but he didn't believe in it. I didn't understand and nobody talks about it.*

🐚 Prescribe tranquilizers or antidepressant medications in the hope that the woman will be less upset about intercourse and will be able to "just do it." Obviously, this is a futile approach, for being under the influence of drugs does not cure the condition. And, what about the other penetrations?

🐚 Prescribe numbing creams (local anesthetics) that are applied intravaginally to block sensations during intercourse. This approach usually fails because it does not address or eliminate the fight-or-flight reaction; It does not teach the woman to accept normal sensations of penetration; And it numbs the partner's penis, altering the reality of intercourse.

🐚 Insisting on performing a pelvic exam despite the woman's panic and anxiety, or dismissing her in an all-too-familiar fashion as told in the following testimonial: *Mom took me for my first gynecological exam. There was no consultation with the doctor before the exam, I just was told to get undressed, put the gown on, and lie down on the examining table. I saw a small picture of Tom Cruise on the ceiling—I was in shock! Did they expect me to enjoy the exam?*

The doctor finally came in and I thought, "Oh good, it's a woman." Women should understand the nervousness of a first-time patient. Boy, was I wrong. She very quickly explained what she was going to do. As she began to insert the speculum, I felt extreme pain and asked her to stop. She made a very rude noise and told me she would have to find a child's speculum. When she returned, she told me grow up and relax. That did not work to help me relax! She was unable to perform the exam. I left the office completely distraught. What was wrong with me? She never told me.

🍃 Offering to do a gynecologic exam under anesthesia, which allows the physician to provide the patient with medical conclusions, but not with any resolution to her vaginismus. What about next year's exam? What about the other penetrations?

🍃 Stretching the vagina is a popular idea— stretch it for ten or even thirty minutes, and she will be able to have intercourse. This is not only inappropriate because vaginismus is not a structural deformity of narrowness, but because it adds to the emotional distress while failing to address the other penetrations. James wrote:

I grew up in a large family and always thought of myself as being open to discussions about anything, including the relationship between a man

*and a woman. Although I understood the impor-
tance of living a chaste life, I was ignorant as to
what a sexually active life would be like. Therefore,
I was shocked and somewhat sick when I found out
that my wife, Beth, had to be "stretched" before we
were married. I was not emotionally equipped to
help her through this time. She knew that she
needed to schedule an appointment with her
gynecologist but she was reluctant to do so. I felt
she had a good reason not to. The appointment was
arranged and I accompanied her there and waited
nervously in the waiting room. While I was waiting, a nurse came out and asked me to rush down
to the pharmacy to fill a prescription for Demerol
and numbing medication. I had no clue at that
time that this would be used to numb her vagina
and to also help her relax for the stretching. After
the whole ordeal, she was given a plastic dilator
and was advised to insert it daily. This was to
prepare herself for our wedding night. I felt so frustrated and confused. I felt somewhat responsible for
Beth's pain. I was even more frustrated when Beth
had to schedule another appointment with her
gynecologist and be restretched, this time without
any Demerol. Outwardly, I gave my full support to
Beth, but inwardly, I feared that I would only hurt
her on our wedding night.*

When asked, Beth gave her account of this
experience:

*I looked forward to being intimate, but I did not
look forward to having intercourse. I was terrified.*

I had bladder infections and bladder surgery as a preadolescent and I had kept horrible memories of the many catheters that I had and the several unsuccessful catheterization attempts. I couldn't imagine intercourse being anything different than the pain I felt in doctors' offices and hospitals. I went to my gynecologist before we got married, and he tried to help me overcome my fears. He gave me Demerol and stretched me with a dilator. It was painful, but I was relieved that I was now "fixed" and would have a beautiful honeymoon. He sent me home with the dilator and told me to insert it once a day until I got married. I couldn't do it! It was too painful for me. I had never inserted anything into my body, not even a tampon. I went back to my doctor a week before I got married, and he stretched me again, but this time he did not give me any Demerol. The pain was so tremendous that I thought I would pass out. Again, he told me to go home and insert the dilator once a day. And again, I couldn't do it. Throughout our engagement, I kept hoping and praying that everything would just "work out" on our honeymoon . . . that somehow, we would be able to have intercourse.

🦐 Opting to perform artificial insemination (under anesthesia) and to deliver a baby by cesarean section ("C" section) instead of vaginal delivery—common themes that reinforce both the ignorance and the frustration in the medical field regarding this condition. The facts remain that couples want to conceive the natural way, and that vaginal delivery is not a contraindication to vaginismus. These misconceptions remind us of an inquiry by a husband who told us that his wife was artificially inseminated following many years of an unconsummated marriage, and their baby was born by a C-section. Now, years later, they are seeking treatment because both are emotionally distraught over the fact that although they are parents, they are still virgins, and the marriage was never consummated.

Performing a hymenectomy—a surgical procedure to remove the hymen—is largely believed to be *the solution*. This misconception is of monumental implications for the clinician, the patient, and her partner. For the clinician, it affords a solution to not being able to otherwise do a pelvic exam, similar to the exam under anesthesia which was previously mentioned. The idea of a hymenectomy comes up because physicians all too commonly presume that the woman cannot have an exam because of a thick hymen! But how can they make this assumption without physically assessing for its accuracy? Maybe she has no hymen left? And why would the woman be so scared of the pelvic exam if all she has is a thick hymen? Has the doctor talked to the woman to find out if she can have any of the other five penetrations? Would it not be in both the doctor and the patient's best interest to see a vaginismus specialist before subjecting her to surgery? This is when diagnosing vaginismus gets lost in favor of a quick medical solution for a conclusive pelvic exam, while avoiding the emotional and sexual crises that are the core of the problem. The surgery promises to "open" the Introitus (vaginal opening), facilitate penetration, and bring about consummation of the marriage. The truth, as patients will confess when encouraged to overcome their feelings of inadequacy and shame, is that while surgery eliminates genital tissue (body), it does not address the fear or the fight-or-flight response associated with penetration (mind), leaving vaginismus intact yet with the added trauma of surgery, failed expectations, and body alterations. Ironically, many of our patients refused to subject themselves to a hymenectomy only to find out, once in treatment with us, that they did not even have any hymen left to be operated on. Lastly, some physicians will repeat the surgery "to make sure it works," while others tell women to make sure to have intercourse as soon as possible after surgery or else the hymen will grow back—what an amazing medical fallacy!

The need to better understand the nature and impact of vaginismus is the key to being able to provide a cure through a well-defined, predictable, and reliable treatment approach. The emotional anguish that is being experienced by the woman mandates competency on the part of the clinician to minimize further disappointments and false hopes. Fragmented, incomplete intervention may offer some explanations, but overall it stirs up more anger and frustration and deepens the sense of helplessness and hopelessness.

Because vaginismus-related hymenectomies are performed so often, we chose to include the following selection of testimonials aimed at educating both professionals and the public about the impact of this unnecessary surgery on the woman and her partner:

Tara's story:

When my husband mentioned to my gynecologist that vaginismus might be our problem, we found that she too was uneducated about it. Her only idea of a solution was surgery. Just the thought of surgery was piercing, but I was determined that this would be the fix. The surgery was called a hymenectomy. It would entail the cutting in four places (2 o'clock, 4 o'clock, 8 o'clock and 10 o'clock positions), and then stitching them back to make the hymeneal ring open. Four nights before the surgery, Mike was searching on the Internet for anything on vaginismus and found the Women's Therapy Center. He tried to do everything he could to get me to talk to them but I wasn't about to let anyone talk me out of the hymenectomy. I was determined the surgery would be the fix. About a month later, I e-mailed The Women's Therapy Center in tears, telling them that I am finally ready to ask for help. That I now understand that this isn't something I can fix myself or just move past; that I can't keep going on like this; that it is truly beginning to affect our marriage;

that we end up fighting almost every night; that we have the perfect marriage until it comes to the bedroom scene. Please help. Help me to conquer the fear, and make the pain go away. It took everything in me that night to ask for help. I was so ready to give up at that point. I felt as if there was no hope.

And Mike's story:

The following day she had the hymenectomy. The gynecologist that performed the procedure told Tara and me that she had excised some tissue, performed the hymenectomy, completed the internal exam inserting three fingers, and performed a pap smear. The pain Tara had for the next week or so was extreme and we had to abstain from any attempts or heavy petting for one month. Just two to three days after the surgery, I knew that it had not been successful. Tara was still unable to touch herself even to apply her medication through an applicator into her vaginal canal. At the end of the first month, at the first evaluation after her surgery, she was still unable to have an external or internal exam without completely breaking into tears in pain.

From another husband:

At one point in our relationship, my wife, using an incredible amount of will, fought her anxiety and visited a gynecologist. Her experience was simply terrifying, but she managed to get through the visit. While she was there, the doctor immediately recommended that my wife needed surgery to correct her condition. This surgery, which we eventually learned was totally useless, was an extremely difficult procedure for my wife to endure, but she bravely fought her anxiety and got through it. Unfortunately, the surgery didn't cure her condition; but her willingness to find a cure, at any cost, continued to reaffirm my faith in her desire to have intercourse. After the surgery was over, the doctor came out to the waiting area to tell me that my wife was fine. He explained the procedure and stated that both he and his surgical assistant had inserted two fingers into my wife's vagina to prove that she was now large enough. I thanked him and he then shook my hand, looked me dead in the eye, and said that although I was an extremely patient person, this problem wouldn't have happened if I were a real man.

Why live with "What's that?"

My spouse and I were both virgins when we married. We were not very well acquainted with each other. We were introduced to each other by family and friends and decided to take the plunge. We expected a lot on the wedding night, nearly six years ago. I thought I was being realistic, expecting a little discomfort and pain. My husband expected to penetrate me with a little trial and error.

For the first few months we fumbled around, expecting to get it right any day. But we were disappointed time and time again. My husband felt that he was trying to push past a stone wall each time he tried. I felt that he was trying, but in the wrong place. Gradually, we ignored this problem and tried to pleasure each other by caresses, kisses, massages, and orally. Oral sex has never been something that I wished for, nor did I enjoy performing it. Yet there was no other place for us to go.

Doctors! What can I say about my experiences with them? The first doctor I went to prescribed mood elevators and sedatives (Zoloft) to relax me enough so that my husband could accomplish the deed. The second doctor I went to said that my pelvic muscles were too strong and suggested that I try a sex therapist. The sex therapist listened to my husband's and my version of the problems we faced and suggested relaxing my body with wine, massages, candlelight dinners, soft porn videos, and hot baths. Basically, her advice was to romance our way into intercourse. Roses, perfume, and wine did not have any effect on me. The third gynecologist asked me to use tampons for a few months, hoping that I would get comfortable with the feeling of something penetrating me. This did not help. I could get the tampons in, but that was it. The fourth gynecologist I went to asked me to use dilators for eight weeks. The doctor also performed a hymenectomy to facilitate penetration.

I was totally confused at this point. The wine and the video advice indicated to me that my problem was mental; the surgery and the dilators indicated to me that my problem was physical. What was I to believe? Which method of treatment should I pursue? I broke down in front of the doctors in every session. None of them suggested that I suffered from vaginismus. I tried to research on the Internet for problems with "women's sexual health." Material about vaginismus was so inadequate that I was unable to match the description of the condition with my problem.

Meanwhile, this problem started taking its toll on our marriage. I dealt with the problem by consulting one doctor after another. My husband dealt with the problem by ignoring it even existed. I resented the fact that he would not come to the doctors with me. He adamantly refused to spend even ten minutes on researching our situation. I was so miserable, knowing that he spent more time researching directions on the Internet than on finding the right doctors. Frequently, I quit trying to actively pursue a solution because he displayed no understanding of the repercussions of our problem. My husband's reason in remaining indifferent to solving the problem was that he felt I was not physically affectionate toward him. How could I tell him that I could not summon up enough enthusiasm to initiate a process that always ended so fruitlessly.

I threw myself into a social life to escape the situation with my husband. But I could not get rid of the problem. It began dominating my every thought. I could no longer relax and be myself. My interest in schooling, hobbies, and career took a backseat as I worried about this problem constantly. When my friends talked about their sex life, I joined in, though I felt upset that I had to lie about what was going on. My terror grew as my age advanced and I faced the prospect of remaining a virgin and childless for the rest of my life. Divorce loomed in my head all along, though I did not know how that would solve the problem. I felt extremely miserable and alone.

Five years of marriage had passed, and I faced strong family pressure to have children. How could I explain the problem to the family? The pressure of keeping this secret from everyone was costing me emotionally. I was constantly bombarded with questions from my family, my husband's family, our friends and relatives about why we were not having children. I started talking less and less to family, to avoid answering this question. My friends were all busy having babies. This depressed me further. Everyone offered me advice on why having children early was important. They suggested fertility treatments. I started feeling boxed in. I avoided going to visit my relatives to escape their curiosity and well-meaning questions.

My five-year wedding anniversary, my advancing age, and my being surrounded by pregnant friends compelled me to seek another doctor. I decided to go in for artificial insemination. My reasoning for going in for the process was twofold: I would not only have a child, but a natural childbirth would enlarge my vaginal canal, allowing me to have sex. I knew I was gambling on having a natural childbirth. I underwent one insemination, and unfortunately (fortunately?) I did not get pregnant. I decided to try again the following month. The doctor said my chances of success were eighty percent of eight tries. Meanwhile, I asked the doctor whether there were any specialists he knew who had treated this problem exclusively. I was given a Website address that was devoted to problems with the vagina.

Wading through the huge list of Websites, I chanced upon the Women's Therapy Center site. This was the only site that had testimonials from patients, and some of the descriptions seemed close to home. I contacted them and the rest is history.

What impressed me most was that for the first time, I felt someone really understood my problem. My optimism increased as they mentioned that they had treated patients who had spent more than ten years in *an unconsummated marriage. I also felt that they talked about the problem realistically. They asked me to hold off the insemination until they had had a chance to treat me. I struggled with that decision. I wanted to try both at the same time, but they convinced me to devote a couple of months to this treatment. The lubrication methods they taught me were so effective and simple that I find it unbelievable that gynecologists did not suggest this to me.*

They did not hesitate in letting me know that I would not really enjoy sex for the first few times when sex would be quite clinical for both my husband and me. At this point, I had no interest in experiencing pleasure. I just wanted to feel normal and less of a freak. My husband joined me for one of the sessions. I am happy to say that I no longer have an unconsummated marriage.

The only thing I have to say to anyone experiencing this problem is, don't bury the problem, hoping that it will go away. I feel anger at the thought I spent several fruitless years looking for a solution that turned out to be so amazingly simple in the end. I think a fully committed spouse would have been very instrumental in helping me find a solution faster. However, if a spouse shows reluctance in actively looking for a solution with you, don't be affected by their lack of support. You have to help yourself overcome this problem.

CHAPTER THIRTEEN

How Do Teen Girls Perceive Their Bodies?

So far, the content of this book discussed vaginismus, including real-life testimonials from women and their partners who experienced the condition firsthand.

Despite the prevalence of the condition, not every woman suffers from it; in fact, most women do not have any problem with any of the five penetrations.

We decided to "visit" where vaginismus begins for many women—during the teenage years, when penetrations first emerge, and when feelings and perception about the body and sexuality become a reality. To do that, we planned a study and gave the assignment to two female teens, each fifteen years old at the time, who volunteered to carry out the interviews equipped with lead questions we gave them, and to summarize their finding in a report format.

The following is their completed project, in its original version.

Thank you, Whitney and Sloane for believing in this project. We are proud of your courage and candidness despite the personal nature of the topic. We are so happy to have you on our team, working together with us in promoting female adolescents' and women's health!

❦ ❦ ❦

How Do Teen Girls Perceive Their Bodies?
by Whitney Sara Sinowitz
and Sloane Jacylyn Tabisel

A group of ten girls, ages thirteen to eighteen, talked about their thoughts and opinions about their bodies.

Periods: We found that most of the girls learned about their periods from their parents, school, friends, siblings, and TV. A fifteen-year-old in the group thinks it is natural, while a thirteen-year-old hates having her period; meanwhile the eighteen-year-old hates it and feels dirty when she has her period. The rest of the group does not like having it either because of the cramps and bloating.

The idea of tampons: We talked to them about how they felt about using tampons and when they felt they were ready to use them. Most of the girls said anywhere from age twelve to sixteen, and one of the girls felt uncomfortable using them alto-gether. The girls said most of their friends, whether at cheerleading, camp, or a slumber party, told them about the use of tampons and influenced them to try it too.

Inserting tampons: We started discussing whether putting tampons in was hard or easy. Most of them said the first time was scary, but after that was fine. One fifteen-year-old said *At first it was a little scary, but after two or three times it's fine.* Some of the fourteen-year-olds were a little cautious about using them, except for one who was okay with it, and uses them regularly. The major-ity of the girls said they do not have trouble getting the tampon in them.

How to teach tampon use? Some of the girls were unsure of how to teach other girls to use them, while some told them to read the box with directions on it and others said they would talk them through it.

Why not use tampons? We asked the girls who did not use tampons why they didn't. A four-teen-year-old said, *I tried it before and it hurt when I put it in. I was also afraid about the things I heard like TSS* (toxic shock syndrome, ed.). Three out of the ten girls said that they do not use tampons and will not try it because they are scared of TSS. Another girl said she did not know why she felt scared, but she did. An eighteen-year-old said, *I just don't like putting them in, and I feel uncomfortable; but if I had to, I would.*

Comments from the authors of this chapter:

We don't understand how tampons could be a negative thing. We feel that they are so much more comfortable and easier to deal with than regular sanitary napkins. The girls that don't use tampons should try to use one because they will realize how easy and how much more comfortable it is. Things like TSS should only scare you if you don't take care of your body. But since both of us do not have negative feelings about our bodies, we are willing to try things and ask questions if we run into problems.

Gynecologic exam: A fifteen-year-old started another conversation about gynecological exams. She said that she probably would be scared the first time, and some of the girls agreed with her. A lot of girls think that having an exam is somewhat disgusting and would feel extremely awkward. One of the fourteen-year-olds said, *I would be a little uncomfortable at first, but a lot more comfortable if it were a woman doctor.* Two of the girls said they would want a woman rather then a man because they would feel more comfortable, thinking that a woman would understand if you were embarrassed at your first exam, has the same parts as you, and knows where you're coming from.

Looking: Would you look at your genitals if you had an itch or a pimple? This is one of the questions that came up in our discussion, and the responses were mostly "no" with the exception of three who said "yes." An eighteen-year-old said, *I would because if it looked abnormal I would want a* *doctor to look at it.* One of the girls shared a story with us about the time when she was thirteen and she thought she had a pimple in her vaginal area. So she called Ditza Katz, Women's Therapy Center, about it and was told to take a mirror into the bathroom and look at herself to see what it was. She was not afraid to look and see what it was; on the contrary, she was able to describe it clearly, apply the suggested cream, and was quickly cured. This is an example of how, if you're not scared to do certain things, you are only helping yourself.

Treating vaginal infections: The question was, if you had a yeast infection, and you had to put an applicator with medication in the vaginal area, could you do it? The predominant answer was "not sure." The fifteen-year-old stated, *I don't know if I would be able to, I'd much rather take a pill or something if it was available.*

Intercourse: The topic of intercourse came up, with questions like do you think it would be painful the first time? Or, when would you lose your virginity? As a rule, the girls thought it would be painful the first time, while a couple thought it wouldn't be that bad. To sum up what the girls said about what they heard about sex, they basically said it is natural to do it with someone you care about, to use protection, to know the person so you don't contract an STD (sexually transmitted disease), and that it is good but can be dangerous if you do not use protection and you are unfamiliar with the person. A thirteen-year-old stated, *I have heard that the first time it does hurt and that it's not*

223

as good as everyone says it is. More or less the girls heard about sex from their moms, teachers, TV, health class, the Internet, movies, friends, and older siblings. Most of the girls said you should be at least over seventeen years old to engage in sexual intercourse or be married. One of the members shared her thoughts on this topic, saying, *I don't think age matters with intercourse. On second thought, actually it does, I don't think a fifteen-year-old should be having sex. However, I don't think there is a set age on when someone should be sexually active. I think if you are in love with someone and feel comfortable with them, then you could have intercourse if you wanted. You should not feel obligated to have sex by a certain age if you don't feel comfortable with your partner.* What you need to feel, always, is comfortable with your body and that you are doing what you want and in no way are forced to do anything you do not want to do.

Talking to parents: Many of the girls particularly said that they would be able to talk to their parents about any sexual questions they might have. One girl said, *My mom and I are very close and we talk about everything. So if I had a sexual question I would feel comfortable asking her about sex and other sexual things.* As some girls do feel comfortable, others either do not or say that it depends on their relationship with their parents. One of the group members stated that *It depends on the question, it might be better to ask someone else like a friend or something.* Girls are usually open with any topic of conversation including that of sexual discussion with other girlfriends.

Intimacy and Sex: The next question was, Do you think that intimacy and sex are a natural part of life? A lot of the responses were yes. They said it was a way to express your feelings for your partner. In order to have an intimate relationship with someone, it does not mean you necessarily have sex. Intimacy shows warmth and a sense of love in a family.

Conclusion: Concisely, many teens perceive their bodies as a natural part of life. As you can see, these teens had no problems expressing themselves and their opinions on different things that all women must think about eventually. Most of the girls were not scared to explore their bodies and try new things, such as using a tampon for the first time. In this day and age, many girls have the same views on sexual activities and values. We can already see in some of the responses from the girls that later on in life, they may have some problems talking about their bodies, or exploring their bodies themselves. We think that our generation is more open to talk about these kinds of things, because we know that it's something that all women go through at some point, and it's nothing to be ashamed of.

We feel grateful that as teens, we can express ourselves and explore our bodies. We know that if we had concerns, we could talk about it to a doctor or parents openly, unlike some of the patients that Ross and Ditza treat that are scared and frightened to do so. It is sad to think that some women are programmed to have negative thoughts about their bodies, and we wish they could feel like we do.

CHAPTER FOURTEEN

Yes, There Is a Cure for Vaginismus!

*L*ife with vaginismus is painful, both physically and emotionally, and understanding the condition is as important to the sufferer as finding a treatment that will bring about a cure. To make this hope come true to every woman who suffers, vaginismus must be brought out into the open, and interested professionals must come forward and be trained to become specialists in the management of this condition.

This chapter is devoted to discussing principles of effective treatment, patients' involvement, and the professional commitment that is needed to treat vaginismus. Also presented in this chapter is our body-mind team concept, the **DiRoss Treatment Approach,** which has a ninety-five percent cure rate.

Regrettably, the content of this chapter is not a self-help instruction manual for the woman or her partner, as vaginismus is too complex to be treated in the privacy of one's own home. Curing the condition requires competent intervention by a specialist, in a face-to-face setting, where the treatment process will be individualized to the particular needs of each patient. Although the general treatment principles are the same in all cases, there are variations that depend on the unique presentation of each situation. In other words, treatment should never be a "one-size-fits-all" approach!

Likewise, this book is not a training module for professionals who wish to become vaginismus specialists. There is no "quick fix" for vaginismus, and this publication is not about teaching a technique or two. Instead, professional training must be done through proper educational seminars, beginning at the basic level and progressing to advanced levels of competency before one may be considered a vaginismus Specialist. Attempting to provide treatment without proper training often results in emotionally scarred patients who continue to suffer from vaginismus, feeling even more helpless and hopeless. However, alternatively to becoming a specialist, being attuned to diagnosing vaginismus and making an appropriate referral to a specialist will prove to be excellent patient care!

We hope that individuals and professionals alike will appreciate the information that is presented in this chapter and will be able to make better choices about treatment options.

The first step in the treatment process must be giving the condition its proper name—vaginismus. There is a great sense of relief that is always experienced by the sufferer once she finds out that there is a medical term for her problem, and that she is not imagining or faking it. In addition to this legitimization, having a name gives the problem a sense of direction, a measure of control over a situation that otherwise may appear quite hopeless: *We were visiting my family doctor regarding a virus I had and we randomly asked him, "Hey Doc, do you know why we can't have intercourse?" We explained the situation and he told us that it sounded like vaginismus. We welcomed this news because at least we now knew what we needed to treat.*

However, knowing the name for the problem is not always enough to initiate treatment. Although there are many women who are eager to "get going" and do not delay the process, there will be just as many who wait years before actually making an appointment. This hesitation is because it takes tremendous emotional strength to overcome the fear of facing the problem, to overcome past disappointments, and to keep the glimmer of hope alive. *My wife acknowledged that she was suffering from this condition but, most importantly, couldn't find the energy to get help. The years of suffering in silence, the pain of a surgery that gave us false hope, and the fear that we might never find a cure all conspired against us.* Some women will seek help because they are facing another force that is bigger than their own fear of vaginismus: the threat of a breakup of the relationship. Others seek help to appease their partners, or because their partner made an appointment for them. Ideally, the reason for seeking treatment should be the woman's desire to own her body and to be able to have **The Five Penetrations of Life**—to be "normal," for herself first.

Women who begin treatment need to make a commitment and show willingness to learn about their body even if the thought repels or frightens them. They need to be able to follow the guidance of the treating professional, and to allow their fears and stress to unfold in order to be helped. Throughout the process they will exchange their "vaginismus control" for a healthier one, that of trusting their body and their knowledge about it, without having the need to enlist fight-or-flight to speak up for them.

Here is what Tara wrote in her diary:

> *I was so nervous as I walked into the therapy center for the first time, but I knew that this was my last resort and that if I truly wanted to be cured, I had to give it my all. So, I put on my "cool head" and told them I was ready to be a new woman.*

If the woman is in a relationship, the partner becomes a factor in the equation, bringing along his or her own coping mechanisms and emotional struggles with the condition. Naturally, a participating partner will be an asset to the process, providing support, encouragement, and unity. Conversely, as was mentioned in an earlier chapter, some women who suffer from the condition enter compromised relationships and stay with them because they feel so inadequate. As the treatment process makes them emotionally stronger and sexually confident, they are able to face the truth about their coping tools from the past and the relationships that came out of them, and make the necessary changes. Vaginismus is indeed not just about sex—it is about life, self-worth and fulfillment.

Choosing the treating professional may not be an easy step, nor should it be taken lightly. The woman and/or her partner must carefully explore their options and take pains in verifying credentials and competency, just as when selecting any other professional for any other problem. If possible, the woman should arrive for the initial appointment having educated herself about vaginismus, then engage with the clinician in a constructive discussion about the condition and suggested treatment process in order to validate her choice.

From the clinician's point of view, treating vaginismus should be a career choice, considering the intricate and intimate nature of the process. Clinicians who wish to specialize in treating vaginismus should be attuned to body language, and possess in-depth knowledge of the body and its function, with emphasis on body-mind interaction. They must also feel comfortable within themselves about physical closeness, touch, sexuality, intimacy, emotional balance, and compassion in order to secure a sense of comfort and confidence in the patient. Their views should be unbiased, and they should be able to step "out of the box," to be non-traditional, yet maintain professionalism.

Resisting any biased opinions, we nevertheless believe that the treating clinician be a female to ensure an understanding "from within" of what it feels like to be a woman, of what it is like to experience penetrations, and what it means to be "entered" or "done to." Another reason for this preference is the intimate nature of vaginismus, making patients reluctant to allow a male clinician into that private zone. Our clinical experience has proven this choice over and over, hearing women state their absolute preference for a female clinician, and their intuitive rejection of a male as a guide for problems involving penetrations, intimacy, and sexuality. However, male physicians should not feel ousted: Once a cure is reached and the woman feels "normal," she is more open to the option of having a male as her regular physician.

From the clinician's point of view, the office setup requires careful planning: Only one patient should be seen per session (approximately one hour), with the specialist/team in direct contact for the duration of the treatment. Initial interview, meeting with patient and partner, and any structured counseling should take place in a comfortable family-room-like setting, which will radiate warmth and a personal atmosphere to help with easing the patient's feelings about exposing her condition. The actual hands-on treatment needs to be rendered in a separate room that will provide visual and auditory privacy from the rest of the office, including an adjacent bathroom for the patient's use during and after treatment. Additionally, it is highly recommended that the décor be pleasant and non-alarming and void of anatomical posters, which may add to the already-stressed state of the patient. An adjustable treatment bed, preferably without stirrups, and fresh linens will add to the sense of comfort and privacy. Of utmost importance is confidentiality—the receptionist and the staff must be trained to be respectful and discreet.

The ideal intervention is that of touching the body and the mind at the same time, rendered by a team consisting of a hands-on vaginismus specialist (physician, physical therapist, nurse, etc.) and a psychotherapist/sex therapist vaginismus specialist. Treatments are intense and uninterrupted, with both specialists present in the treatment room for the duration of the session so that any emotional or physical problem can be addressed right on the spot, without fragmentation. However, until such teams of vaginismus specialists are the standard of care, the hands-on specialists and the psychotherapy/sex therapy specialists should work together by cross-referrals in order to provide as much continuity of care as possible.

The treatment itself is not about sexual skills or how to be sexy. As a matter of fact neither sexual feelings nor sexual stimulation are a part of the process. Instead, a realistic view of the facts is the guide: In primary vaginismus, the vaginal canal is truly virgin, void of kinematic (touch) experience and memory. In cases of secondary vaginismus and dyspareunia, the vagina and the brain retain a negative imprint of penetration, one that is in need of reformatting into the positive.

Just like a developing infant establishes brain mapping of the body parts by way of repetitious touch and repetitious activities, so are the genitals and the vagina in need of establishing familiarity with various touches within it and around it, including different textures, volumes, and pressures, similar to what a woman would experience vaginally in the course of a healthy life.

The ideal, proven treatment for vaginismus is a *guided tour* of the woman's genitals in general and of the vagina in particular, including the teaching of **The Five Penetrations of Life.** The guides are the clinicians who offer explanations, demonstration, hands-on practice, and the necessary emotional intervention. The need for guidance is why this condition cannot be treated by the woman herself in the privacy of her own home, and why she cannot just "relax and let it happen."

Since vaginismus is a body-mind phenomenon, it must be treated through both, the body and the mind, by following these general guidelines:

🐚 Medical (psychophysical) management of vaginismus, including explanation of the condition and its etiology (causes), diffusing the fight-or-flight reaction, and teaching the five penetrations.

🐚 Psychological management of inadequacy, hopelessness, betrayal of hopes, disappointment, etc., to the patient, and her partner when possible.

🐚 Identifying and eradicating the negative coping mechanisms, such as avoidance of intimacy, starting a fight right before bedtime, overworking, somatization, living in secrecy, infidelity, separation, etc.

🐚 Clarifying misconceptions about sexual practice and sexual needs of men versus women, the role of men versus women in the sexual arena, and sexual fantasy (movies, books) versus reality. Included in this area are sex education and sex therapy, and ensuring that partners can state their preferences and wishes, never feeling forced into any situation.

🐚 Exploring birth control, sexually transmitted diseases, pregnancy planning, and family pressure to have children.

The **DiRoss Treatment Approach** is the result of our pioneering efforts to establish a well-defined, methodical, and result-oriented intervention to vaginismus. It is a "hands-on, hands-in, hand-in-hand" approach that takes the woman through physical, mental, and emotional penetration training. It encourages the woman to explore her body despite feeling inadequate and abnormal. It reverses the longstanding negativity about the body and the self. It takes the woman through hundreds of practices in order to gain proficiency of penetrations. It establishes positive brain memory for penetrations by making them simple and painless. Lastly, the **DiRoss Treatment Approach** brings physical and emotional integration, and facilitates a smooth transition to healthy womanhood and sexual intimacy.

The general outline of our process looks like this:

Patient interview regarding the nature of her problem, including input from the involved partner if available. Also examined are the patient's medical history, obstetric history, nutrition, exercise habits, personal history, living arrangements, and sexual history.

Patient education of her pelvis using a three-dimensional model with removable internal organs for ease of visualization and clear understanding, followed by actual demonstration on her own body of her external genitals. Explanations also include menstruation, ovulation, conception, birth control methods, the location and function of the pelvic floor musculature, mechanisms of voiding and defecation, sexually transmitted diseases, and a breast exam. Not all patients feel comfortable moving on to this "being touched" phase; this is where the body-mind approach is put to work in helping to overcome this reluctance.

More from Tara's journal:

The first treatment was great for me. Anatomy 101. I was raised in a very religious home and went to a private high school; sex was never a topic that was discussed during my adolescence. I was absolutely clueless when it came to the human body. Of course I knew a man had a penis and a woman had a vagina, but those were just words to me. To think that the clitoris was anything but excess skin was amazing, let alone be arousing to a woman. Then Ditza, Ross, and myself went into the exam room where they held a mirror and pointed out each item on my body and touched it either with a finger or a Q-tip so I knew where it was and what it felt like. Then they had me do the inevitable . . . touch those parts myself. I hated the idea of touching myself. But it actually did me a lot of good; I realized that it doesn't hurt to be touched, and it wasn't gross . . . but just a different feel that I was not used to.

Guided tour of the vagina: demonstrating, teaching, practicing, and proofing **The Five Penetrations of Life** in the office, under direct guidance: finger, applicator, tampon, intercourse simulation, and gynecologic exam (speculum insertion, Pap smear practice, manual exam, breast exam, and rectal exam). Penetrations are practiced by the patient into herself, as well as by the hands-on specialist who performs the penetrations into the patient for simulation of being "done to." Following each treatment session, the patient is given specific homework exercises to be done at home in order to develop proficiency of the acquired penetration.

Each treatment session also includes panic and anxiety management while the body is experiencing the different penetrations. Additional teachings and practice include how to use lubrication, how to handle tampons and vaginal applicators, what is included in a gynecologic exam, etc.

More from Tara's journal:

That day I was able to put in my very first tampon. Never before had I been able to use a tampon, this was the start of a new me. I could now go swimming and not have to worry about being the only one sitting out in my shorts when everyone knew why. I didn't have to wear "diapers" [pads] anymore.

Having intercourse is the next major step in the process, as Howard writes:

So, here we are one day before we are supposed to have intercourse for the first time in our seven-year marriage. I am very excited about the opportunity to finally consummate our marriage. Not just from the sexual aspect of having intercourse, but from the psychological aspect for both my wife and me. We have a very strong marriage, built on love and trust that goes beyond the sexual part of a relationship. However, the need to feel like a normal husband and wife is very powerful. We would constantly see other couples younger than us having children while we could not even have intercourse. This became very disheartening. Now I feel that this weight and burden is about to be lifted from our shoulders. I also believe that the sexual part of a marriage is very important, as it creates a very intimate bond between husband and wife, a bond that we have never been able to create or experience. Now, if everything goes as we hope and pray, we will be able to experience this tomorrow, even if only in a clinical way. This is the final culmination of all the effort and hard work that we have done in order to add a normal aspect to our marriage that had been impossible before.

Yes, the first intercourse is done in a rather "clinical" manner because the woman's mind is not at all on being sexually aroused but rather on two basic questions: "WILL HE BE ABLE TO GET IN? WILL IT HURT?" As soon as intercourse happens and she gets her answers, she is ready to move on to integrating intercourse into her sexual repertoire. Typically, having reached this point, the woman will marvel at the ease of penetration during intercourse and at the same time will wonder if this "miracle will happen again," a real question with a simple answer: "Yes, do it again and prove it to yourself!" On another note, a partner who is looking to the first intercourse as finally having that wonderful, passionate moment he was waiting for, may meet this "clinical" setup with quite a bit of resentment because the woman's mind is focused on finding the physical proof that "it works." Therefore, both partners are reminded that although the woman will not be involved sexually, both are involved emotionally in experiencing intercourse together for the first time! In another common scenario, involved male partners who find themselves unable to stay erect for that first (or even second) intercourse because of their own emotional coping with vaginismus are encouraged to keep trying, as the erectile dysfunction is only temporary.

Here is what James wrote:

> *The time was approaching when we were going to have intercourse. Ross and Ditza said that they had repeatedly seen "nice guys" not able to have intercourse because of performance anxiety, and I did not rule that out as a problem I might have. I had seen how much progress Beth had made and I did not want to ruin it. When the time came I was okay with the first intercourse, but sure enough, I didn't feel ready for the second one. It took a couple of more attempts to be able to have that second intercourse because I was not able to have an erection. I still worried about hurting Beth. But she was okay and we made it through.*

Single women, and those who would rather hold off on intercourse until marriage, are given specific instructions for penetration homework, to be done on a regular basis, until intercourse becomes an available option.

Once proficient, the patient is sent to have a gynecologic exam by her attending physician. This is always a gratifying moment, a real proof to both the patient and her doctor that the process was a success.

To complete the process, additional sex education and/or psychotherapy counseling are offered as per the needs of the particular situation.

As was mentioned earlier, no sexual stimulation of any kind is included in the process! Women and vaginas can experience penetration in a neutral way, a fact that is the foundation of the treatment process. Once able to own the five penetrations, the woman can use her body in a neutral way for tampon or medication insertion, in a medical way for pelvic exams, and in a sexual way for intercourse once her mind is free to allow it to happen.

The **DiRoss Treatment Approach** offers permanent repair of vaginismus, at ninety-five percent success, without recurrence. The patient who completes the process is cured for life, able to put the condition behind her and never look back.

From Beth's journal:

> *Our first appointment was full of anxiety. I was imagining all of the terrible things that could possibly go on and made myself physically sick for my appointment. Through our lessons in anatomy and frank discussions about intimacy, I became more comfortable. This was so important to me because they were my last hope of ever curing vaginismus. And so the bodywork began.*
>
> *Within a day, I was able to insert two different spacers that were bigger than any tampon I had ever seen. I worked so hard while I was there. Emotionally, physically, and spiritually, I was exhausted.*
>
> *And then it was our day for intercourse. I knew it was going to work; I just knew it had to. We went straight home from our appointment and had intercourse within half an hour and I couldn't believe it actually happened. The biggest shock to me is that there was no pain. I started to wonder what I had been so afraid of in the past. We called the Women's Therapy Center and then I called my mom and told her I wasn't a virgin anymore. That was the greatest feeling I ever had. We knew that our trial with vaginismus was well on its way to being completely overcome.*

We were both so emotional afterward. I hadn't felt that kind of peace since we had become engaged. The tension was gone. All the fighting about how to handle a marriage without intercourse was slowly fading away, and we could both feel that. I remember going out to the mall that night and not having that feeling of, "We have to run home and start trying to see if this is the night that we can have intercourse." We went through that for three years. For the first time that night, we cuddled as we fell asleep, because it was our choice, not our only option.

We took a second honeymoon to Hawaii a month after we got home from the treatment. It was like a dream. It was so nice to finally have what we had been dreaming about for three years. It was a real honey-moon, with intercourse included this time.

The process changed our lives. Our marriage that had so many wonderful aspects now seems balanced because we have added the aspect of physical love. We are at more peace with ourselves and each other, and we feel like we have had a second chance to start over in our marriage. Looking back at our trial of vaginismus, I can see that we were blessed all along the way with experiences to make us stronger and give us the strength needed to complete the therapy and make the miracle happen.

In summary, it is imperative that the treatment of vaginismus is *not* viewed as physical "stretching" of a tight vaginal canal, or relaxing stiff pelvic floor muscles. Instead, it should be accepted as a progressive journey of processing the kinematic (touch) awareness felt with each new penetration. It is combining bodily sensations with mental visualization in order to establish new neurological connections in the brain for positive and painless penetrations. Through this journey, each penetration becomes a healthy, positive sensation that is anatomically natural and available; and with each positive penetration, there is less triggering of the stress response system, until a complete resolution is attained. Adhering to this concept of treatment will lead to empowerment, and will stop vaginismus from clinging as a title for life.

Paco told us:

Valerie had told me that she had never made love. She was nineteen and I was twenty-five. I already had prior sexual relationships with other girlfriends, and the fact that she was inexperienced did not bother me at all. When we tried to have intercourse the first time, things were a little odd. Valerie became extremely tense and every time I tried to calm her or talk to her, she would not answer. It was as if she had gone to another place and was unable to communicate at all. Her thighs became so tensed up that it was absolutely impossible to have intercourse. She started sweating, and if I tried to push or press in any way, she would just start screaming and crying.

After a few attempts, it became clear that Valerie had a problem. Still, I was really in love with this woman and I figured that we would fix the problem sooner of later.

When I moved to the USA, I learned a lot more about Valerie's past and her upbringing. She was raised in a Catholic environment, and her parents, especially her father, were very strict disciplinarians: church every

Sunday, piano lessons, ballet lessons, study, do not play, etc. Her life had always been written for her and she never had a chance to express herself or to take her own initiatives. Needless to say, having sex, boyfriends, or any type of relationships was totally out of the question. She had to remain a virgin and untouched until marriage. She never once heard a word about sex from her parents other than the warnings of how bad sex was and how bad a person she would be if she ever pronounced the word sex, let alone actually have it.

After learning all of that, I thought that the best way for us to get over this problem was to get married, so Valerie could move out of her parents' house. That way the treatment would be free of the obstacles that we had at that time. We got married three years after we met. No need to say that our wedding night was a disaster, as the other nights had been. Still I thought that now we were free to look for a solution to the problem.

A few months after getting married, we read an article in a magazine in which couples described the same problems we were having. Finally our problem had a name and we were not alone in this. The name was vaginismus, and Valerie had the same symptoms as other sufferers. We started researching on the Internet, learned that the problem was not physical but psychological, and that we should seek the help of a sexual therapist. At this time, our relationship was still strong but Valerie was accumulating a lot of anxiety and tension. She would start laughing out of control, only to cry and be depressed just minutes later. Small things would make her mad to the point of crying. Things were not looking promising at all.

For the next year-and-a-half, we visited several doctors with no results at all. Valerie was still unable to relax and have normal sex. It was beyond her control, and by then I had been about five years without making love. I still loved Valerie but the burden was getting too heavy for me at that point.

The problem with vaginismus sufferers is that the idea of even fixing the problem becomes too uncomfortable for them, because they would have to face it. This was the point that made us take the steps that would eventually help us.

As our second anniversary was nearing, I told Valerie that either we were going to fix the problem or we were splitting up. As much as I loved her, I was not willing to give up my sexual life. I had spent five years already without sex and I thought that that was enough for both of us.

That same night Valerie found the Women's Therapy Center Website on the Internet. At this point we had already talked to her parents, and they were aware of the problem. We scheduled our trip to the Center. Valerie would get there first, and I would meet her three days later.

The first day I got there, I was extremely skeptical. At that point, I believed that Valerie's problem had no real solution and that we would probably split up by the end of the summer. It took me one day to realize how wrong I was. Three days later we made love for the first time.

Neither Valerie nor I would have believed that this problem was ever going to be fixed. One of the major problems with vaginismus is the conspiracy of silence that surrounds it. No one knows about it because sufferers don't talk about it. Thousands of women and their partners are out there waiting to hear the story of somebody like us so they can see that they are not alone. It is ironic that the same thing that creates this problem keeps perpetuating it. First, you suffer from vaginismus because talking about sex is the worst thing in the world, then nobody is aware of vaginismus because you have been trained to be ashamed of it and to keep it quiet.

It is not a shame to suffer from vaginismus or to have a partner that suffers from it. There is a solution for it. It is a medical problem with a reason and an explanation for it.

Vaginismus is what has been done to you, not who you are. There is no reason not to talk about it .

You are no less a woman for suffering from it and you are no less a man for having a partner who suffers from it. After all, it is your problem too.

It has been two months since we came back from the Women's Therapy Center in New York and our sex life is looking more and more normal every day. The most noticeable change, however, is the fact that things are suddenly normal again. Valerie does not have depressions anymore, I do not have mood swings, and we do not have to think about vaginismus anymore. We are now preparing to move back to Spain, where we believe we will have a brand new beginning. Things are looking exciting again, and after working through this problem together, we know that there are few obstacles that we cannot overcome.

CHAPTER FIFTEEN

The Blue Line

This is a true story. It is about owning a personal space and about being confident and self-assured. It is the story of Sloane, a young girl who had difficulties with her father; about how she did not feel she had the right to talk to him about her feelings; and about the advice she followed which changed her life.

We always tell this story because so many people share the same feelings of inadequacy and powerlessness, of not believing that they have the right to their feelings and wishes, regardless of the particular reasons that led them there.

The Blue Line is a "tangible" that describes an abstract; that being the imaginary space that surrounds each of us . . . the line of demarcation that defines who and what we are; the sense that gives us the right to speak up or to say *NO* when necessary; the one that guides us toward establishing personal preferences and, when needed, to act in self-protection.

The Blue Line has become a meaningful gift we give to others, and especially to our vaginismus patients, to inspire courage, confidence, and power. It has made a difference!

The cover of this book brings the Blue Line to you. We hope that you will accept this gift from us, will cherish it, and will pass it along to others.

My Blue Line
by Sloane, age fifteen

The Blue Line started when I was ten years old and was having problems with my dad. At that time my parents were separated and I was living with my mom.

My dad used to always call me up at the last minute to tell me that he was picking me up to go and visit at his house. Sometimes I already made plans to go to birthday parties and could not go with him because he asked me at the last minute. I also knew that he could come for me anytime he wanted, as was agreed between my parents. I wanted to spend time with him . . . But I also wanted to be told ahead of time so that I did not make plans and have to cancel them. After all, at ten, having friends and going to their parties was important to me.

He also used to decide what I was going to do when I was going to visit with him, and he gave me no options. This bothered me a lot and I didn't know how to tell him that I didn't like the fact that I was being told what to do and when to do it without ever being asked if I liked the plans. He did not seem to understand that when I was with him, I wanted to spend time just with him and not share him with others! I was a ten-year-old trying to grow up, and I felt my dad was stopping me from doing that by treating me like a baby.

One night Ditza came over to my mom's house and I asked her for advice on how to tell my dad about my feelings. I wanted him to let me be my own person, and let me make my own decisions.

Ditza told me to pick a color and draw a line of that color. My favorite color was BLUE. . . . So yes, this is where the Blue Line came from! She then told me that this is my Blue Line, and that I live on one side of the line and everyone else, including my parents, live on the other side of the line. She then said that, as the owner of the line, I could let people into my side—my personal area of the line—or tell them to leave. Ditza also said that in life, sometimes people would try to cross that line; but that I can ask them, politely, to leave. This applies even to your own father or mother.

I understood. But I was afraid that my dad wouldn't take it the right way, or might even get angry with me. Ditza reassured me that he is my dad and that he loves me because I am his little girl, and that I must tell him that he is making me upset.

That same night I called my dad. It was so hard for me to tell him that I didn't like the fact that he was making all the decisions for me; that I don't always like where he takes me, or the people that we have to eat with every night when I visit him. I also told him that since I hardly ever get to see him, I don't always want it to be him and me and another person—I want it to be just us spending time together.

He told me that he loves me and that he never meant to hurt me, and he apologized. From this point on, he has always made sure it was okay with me or asked me what I wanted to do over the time I spend with him.

That night affected my whole life, and it always will. It taught a ten-year-old a life lesson: Never let anyone walk over you and never allow anyone to tell you what to do.

Since then, I never let anyone disrespect my friends or myself. This doesn't mean that I am rude to others, it just means I won't let anyone cross my Blue Line. There are also rules that my parents set for me as a teenager that I must respect, like cleaning my room, doing my homework, following my curfew, etc. But I also know that if I believe in something, that I may use my Blue Line to express my opinion. A Blue Line gives one a feeling of inner strength and a sense of self-esteem.

Today, as a fifteen-year-old, I know I can express my feelings and speak my mind freely on any issue, knowing that it's okay. I share the information of how to never let anyone tell you what to do with all my friends. A lot of them don't realize that it's "okay to say no and I don't want to do something." They don't realize that it is their body and their mind and no one can tell them what to do if they don't want to do it. The concept of having your own mind, or a say in what you want to do, can never be taken away from a person.

For example, I have friends that smoke, yet I am able to tell them not to do it in front of me because my belief as an individual is that I do not want to smoke and ruin my life just because everyone else does. If they want to follow the trend and say how much they like it, they may try to use peer pressure on me; but that doesn't mean that I have to smoke or do anything like that. As a teen I guess it's hard because everyone wants to fit in and be popular, but that doesn't mean you have to do things you don't want to do just because everyone is doing it.

When I was younger, I didn't want to share my Blue Line. I remember sitting in a restaurant with Ditza and my mom and Ditza told me that she "gave my Blue Line to a patient." I cried and said, "You can't give away my Blue Line!" But now I know that it's inside my heart, and that I can share it and teach others to say no and have a good strong Blue Line.

I hope that this story helps all the patients that have been treated by Ditza and Ross, and as many other people as possible.

A Blue Line gives courage, confidence, and a sense of self-satisfaction to those who need to believe in themselves and allows them to stand tall.

CHAPTER SIXTEEN

Empowerment

- ❦ Knowing the body and understanding how it works.

- ❦ Owning all five penetrations.

- ❦ Believing in yourself.

- ❦ Not being afraid to try new things.

- ❦ Proving that the hope for a cure is a reality.

- ❦ Feeling adequate, capable, and proud.

- ❦ Confident with your own sexuality.

- ❦ Positive about life and relationships.

- ❦ Feeling normal as a woman.

- ❦ Being free of vaginismus!

*E*mpowerment is the outcome of the journey to a cure. It is the result of integrating the questions with the explanations, the fears with penetration practices, the emotional anguish with conquering the condition. Empowerment is reversing the devastation of vaginismus; it is leaving the prison of shame, inadequacy, and pain, and beginning a new life full of hope and promise.

Empowerment begins with understanding that vaginismus is not a failure but a medical condition, then continuing through seeking a solution and undergoing treatment until a complete recovery is reached. Empowerment grows in stages and builds on its own, gaining momentum from one day to the next. It is the engine that strengthens the spirit during the treatment process. Empowerment is the proof that the woman is cured, body and mind.

Each woman experiences empowerment in different ways; combined, these variations cover all facets of life, including her partner and her relationships. The following vignettes, written by patients, former patients, and partners represent the best description of this powerful transformation:

Secrecy and silence about having the condition is typical of most vaginismus sufferers, and is the main reason most feel that they are "the only one who suffers from it." Empowerment reassures that there are many others who have this problem; that the condition affects women of all walks of life and all cultural and religious backgrounds; and that yes, there is a cure for it.

The following is from Ann's diary:

Overall, the treatment included lessons about anatomy as well as physical bodywork and emotional support. The approach was very organized, and it made complete sense to me. I made progress every day, and that boosted my confidence to heights it had never seen before. During the course of treatment, I was able to speak with others who were also treated at the Center and they provided additional comfort and inspiration along the way. This treatment changed my life in more ways than one. I have an in-depth understanding of my body, probably a better understanding than most women who had "normal" sex lives. I can use a tampon. I can—and did—have a successful gynecological exam . . . and, most importantly, I can choose to have intercourse with my husband. Before, the choice was not mine. Today I am fully cured. In fact, not only did we finally consummate our marriage, but during that time, I also became pregnant. You can imagine the joy we felt. We felt like we won on several fronts. While the joy of the pregnancy lasted only for a short time due to an early miscarriage, I know that I am a winner still. I overcame this thing. That, in and of itself, was incredible to us. I no longer dwell on the aspect of my life plagued by vaginismus; rather, I look to the future with great possibility. I have more confidence in my ability and am at peace with my life. On the wall in the treatment room at the Women's Therapy Center hangs a famous painting called The Origin of the World[1]. *It's a portrait of a woman's vagina. I thought to myself then and I think to myself now this is beautiful— this is where it all begins . . . and I have hope.*

---

[1] *L'Origin du monde* by Gustave Courbet, 1866

Getting to know and understand the genitals is a must in order to continue with the treatment process. As was mentioned earlier in the book, the female genitals are usually viewed as a collection of mysterious parts that lead somewhere into the body (pelvis), a perception that harbors scary interpretations and fear of penetration. Empowerment is owning every part of the body and feeling good about it: *I have come a long way from the sixteen-year-old girl who was terrified of everything having to do with her own body. I am very educated about all the relevant parts of my body and I feel like I can handle anything!*

Struggling to find the balance between the painful past and the healthy future may put empowerment to the test, calling on the woman to search deep within herself for that spark of hope and courage to fight the past.

K.C. describes this very feeling:

I knew my fear of pain was all in my head due to the lack of knowledge of my own body. I learned the female anatomy and what happens in our bodies. The hands-on approach helped me get used to the sensation in the area of my body that I wasn't comfortable with. I learned how to use tampons and how to prepare for my first visit to the gynecologist to get a Pap smear. I gained confidence each time. However, the process got hard sometimes and I had mood swings; they were probably because I was putting so much pressure on myself to do well and to be cured quickly, stressing myself out. But I overcame them, and within a short time, I was able to have intercourse with my husband. It was a little surreal, and I went, "Wow, this is it? I'm not scared at all!" Amazingly, my fear of pain had gone away. I couldn't believe the difference. I have been on the pill because we're not planning on getting pregnant yet. For now, our focus is on enjoying sex and life.

Overcoming panic and anxiety is a monumental achievement in the process, altering life for the better in all areas, not only with regard to curing vaginismus. Familiarity with penetrations coupled with being able to speak up and feel confident are the fundamental changes, which then eliminate the need for unnecessarily enlisting the fight-or-flight protective response. Empowerment is being in control, not being controlled!

Here is what Katy wrote about her journey to power:

We had already been married almost three years. I was twenty-five years old and had never been able to have intercourse, wear a tampon, or have a gynecological exam. I had been to different doctors who had all told me that "I needed to relax." By this point, I thought it was all in my head and I was a freak. Once we read the information provided by the Women's Therapy Center, I knew it was not my fault and that I was not alone. It brought a great deal of comfort to me as well as to my husband. Since we live in New Jersey, we made arrangements to stay on Long Island for two weeks. On Monday morning I headed off by myself because my husband had to work. I was a nervous wreck. Going by myself was not something I looked forward to. In hindsight, though, it was the best thing that could have happened. For four days I was by myself and did not have him to coddle me when I was having an anxiety attack. It forced me to get over being scared and do what needed to be done. When he finally came up on Thursday, he did not recognize me. I had become a totally different person. During my sessions I learned that I could not let anxiety take over my life. I learned that if I remained in control, I could do whatever I put my mind to. It was amazing to me how different I felt about life. Monday, eight days later, I was able to have intercourse for the first time. It was amazing how relaxed and easy it was. Then on Tuesday, I was able to have an orgasm for the first time, which was incredible. I had never been able to get to that point before because I always got scared and made my husband stop. This time, though, I just sat back, relaxed, and let him take over. It is amazing what will happen if you just relax. I left Long Island the following Friday feeling like a different woman. It is amazing what this experience will do for your life. I still cannot believe, sometimes, what those two weeks did for my life. Even other family members and friends noticed a changed in my personality. I am much more positive and sure of myself now. This experience is one I will never forget, and I now have a "normal" marriage.

Empowerment evolves throughout the journey to a cure, gaining momentum with each new achievement, with each new revelation. The following was written by Dawn, while still in treatment, as she was beginning to sense the soon-to-arrive happy end:

Tomorrow will be a monumental day in my life, as I will be having sexual intercourse with my husband

and consummating our seven-year marriage. I will feel like a complete person, knowing that I have achieved one of the most natural things that occurs between two people. I know that problems will still arise in my life in the future; however, I feel that after achieving this goal, there will not be any problems that I cannot handle. From the very first time that sexual intercourse was initiated on our wedding night and proved to be unsuccessful, I had always felt that I was different from other women, and abnormal. I didn't know at that time that the condition I suffered from had a name, and was called vaginismus. At first, I tried to put my mind at ease, thinking as time goes along that sexual intercourse would get better. Why wouldn't it, if everybody else can have sexual intercourse? Why not me? How can I be the one person in this world that cannot have sexual intercourse? After one year of marriage and numerous unsuccessful attempts at intercourse, I felt as if maybe there was something wrong with me that I did not know how to fix or have a solution to. Having discovered that my problem did have a name, called vaginismus, I sought therapy from a local psychologist. However, after almost nine months of therapy, I was not cured and still could not consummate my marriage. I felt even more alone and depressed. I started to find more things to do in my life to fill the void with which vaginismus left me. I believed that if I kept myself busy enough with other responsibilities, I would eventually forget the problem. I was carrying a dark deep burden that was unavoidable. One day I realized that my life on earth was not eternal. I only had as much time on earth as everyone else. If

I continued to remain in this pattern of denial, one day I would realize I had wasted too many years of my life and missed a lot of life's opportunities. That is when I discovered The Women's Therapy Center, read the statistics and testimonials many times, and decided it was time to make a difference in my life. Life is too precious to live in fear of vaginismus. I am now at the stage that I will have sexual intercourse for the first time in my life. I am a little anxious but mostly thrilled to know that I can achieve this goal with my husband, who has always been very patient and supportive. I feel mentally and physically prepared to do so. I have learned to believe in myself and to trust my feelings. I am looking forward to finally proceeding to another stage in my life that just a few weeks ago was impossible for me to do. To achieve sexual intercourse will give me the liberation from my fears that have for so long restrained me. For my husband and I, we will finally be able to create a family in our future. Tomorrow will be a milestone in my life. Not only will I have sexual intercourse for the first time, but I will also be able to look into the mirror and see myself as someone I can respect, trust, and love.

The effect of empowerment on the partner cannot be denied. The frustration, anger, helplessness, and hopelessness evaporate, making room for a renewed sense of intimacy, partnership, and dreams for a happy future. We often hear partners describe their reaction as "I cried like a baby when we were able to consummate our marriage," or describing how they were finally able to sleep through the night without worrying and without the stress they have suffered.

This is what one partner wrote:

Today, vaginismus is out of my life and intercourse, lots of it, is in my life and, most importantly, my wife's life. Although going through this process was, hopefully, the hardest thing we'll ever experience, I learned a lot about my wife, our life together, and myself. Most people probably think that it's unfortunate we lost all that time together, but the opposite is truer. What we learned during that time will never leave us and the fact that we learned from this experience has made each of us stronger as individuals and as a couple. In hindsight, we could have gotten help sooner, but I firmly believe that other options would not have worked for us. We had experienced a lot of life together and were enjoying a healthy marriage in every way but one. I never believed that I should throw all that away because of one problem, albeit a gigantic one. I believed in my wife all along, and didn't think I should stop believing or loving because she couldn't will herself to get help. For her, vaginismus was a two-part problem— an inability to have intercourse, and a massive fear of the emotional and physical pain she might have suffered while finding a cure. Before we found our cure together, I believed that my faith in my wife's ability to overcome this problem on her own was a curse. Now, I know it was a blessing. During those years we grew closer, our marriage grew stronger, and we survived an odyssey that I thought would never end. In the end our faith in each other, and our love, got us through a dark period in our lives. Today, our odyssey has ended, our love for each other is as strong as when we first met and our new journey has begun.

The effect on the relationship merges the woman's empowerment with that of her partner, melting away any barriers that were created as a result of coping with vaginismus. Intimacy is resurrected, family planning becomes an available choice, and a sense of normalcy settles in. The following two quotes are from a patient and from the husband of another patient, each describing the effect on their relationship.

S.M. wrote:

When I met my husband, I knew that he was the man I wanted to spend forever with. Waiting until marriage to make love seemed a natural decision. I had saved myself for true love. Our wedding night was my first time, and when the night that had been envisioned as one of pleasure and fulfilled dreams became one of pain and despair, I felt alone and afraid. I continued having intercourse sporadically, causing fights with my husband and feigning illness to avoid it. The burning and pain led to tears and stressful arguments as my self-esteem plummeted. I felt unwanted and alone. I thought that it was all in my head. Then my doctor, seeing my discomfort and fear during my Pap smear, said I might have vaginismus. I was so relieved to learn of the diagnosis that I jumped on the computer and searched the web, which led me to the Women's Therapy Center. The approach of education taught me about my body, leading to feelings of ownership and control. This feeling of control helped me throughout the therapy. I know how to ease my discomfort and have gained more self-esteem. I can use a tampon and was able to have a Pap smear without wincing. I didn't even feel it. The most amazing transformation is my ability to have intercourse and enjoy it. I actually buy myself lingerie and ask my husband to have "couple time." The weeks of therapy were a successful beginning of a new chapter ending a year of suffering."

And James concludes his story, portions of which were presented earlier in the book: *We had become graduates and we loved it. Since then our progress has been continually getting better. We have had our struggles, but we are seeing life in a whole new light. We went to Hawaii for our "second honeymoon" and we were able to rekindle our romantic life. We have had some struggles, but now we look at them as preparing the way for us to be stronger individually and as a couple. Vaginismus wasn't our first struggle and probably won't be our last, but we can honestly say that we are a better couple because of it.*

The sense of liberation to do anything and everything one wishes to try is another inspiring outcome of the healing process, of empowerment. This freedom to experience life in a mature and spontaneous way spills into socialization, work, education, hobbies, and family. A typical message we receive from just about every "graduate" is how their days are now free of tension, how they have so much more energy to focus on the present instead of being consumed by vaginismus. *We can think of other things now and no longer obsess about vaginismus.* Empowerment also gives a woman a change of attitude toward sex in general, and a new way to address the topic with family and with her own children in the future. The following is from a young lady who walked in upset, and walked out, at the conclusion of her treatment, tall and happy:

As for me, I'm doing great. I'm getting adjusted to my new job, and to my new inner awareness of myself. I can't believe how my life has changed. I feel more confident and self-assured of myself. I thought I always had this within me, except for the situation that was going on with me (the vaginismus), but now it's different. I'm no longer reluctant or critical of meeting someone or getting involved with someone because of the fear of becoming intimate.

Physical radiance is quite a noticeable change, whether by way of dressing, putting on makeup and jewelry, losing weight, buying gifts for one's self, or walking in a more confident way. We have seen patients who set aside favorite clothes or gifts they received, saving them to put on when they are cured, and not a moment sooner. A wonderful feeling of empowerment was transmitted by a patient who underwent treatment, having suffered from vaginismus for the entire seventeen years of her marriage. She and her husband had already separated once, then came back together, realizing how much they loved each other despite the inability to consummate their marriage. Still, they were seeking a cure. They also wanted to have children "the natural way." The day after they were able to have their first intercourse, they walked into our office and we hardly recognized her: She was wearing new clothes that she had just bought herself, her makeup was bright and cheerful, and her smile was wide—she was glowing with happiness, as though she had been just reborn.

Becoming advocates for vaginismus, willing to speak on the phone or in front of a camera or microphone about the condition, is another aspect of empowerment. It lifts the shame and stigma that are associated with "sexual failure" or with "being crazy," and replaces them with authority and conviction; with the confidence to say, "Yes, I had that problem. Would you like to learn more about it so that you, too, can be cured?" Nearly all our "graduates" are eager to give back by becoming advocates. They volunteer to come to the office to speak to new patients. They accept phone calls from women who are considering the treatment but wish to first speak with someone who has been there. Some partners will be as willing to speak to other partners and share their experiences. Most "graduates" will make it a point to educate their physicians and their community about vaginismus so that women will no longer have to suffer from this "unknown condition."

The sense of completion envelops empowerment, making it a reality. The feeling of arriving at a final destination of the journey of pain and suffering, and embarking upon a new journey, that of normalcy, is the force that ties the loose ends together. *I can say now that I am totally cured from vaginismus; trying intercourse at home was not a big deal! I even started enjoying it now. I am so excited to start my new life, I feel totally confident and ready to overcome all kinds of difficulties.*

Sexual empowerment integrates all the levels of the being into a harmonious existence, merging physical experiences with emotional and spiritual freedom to feel, communicate, explore, and express. It is the most intense level of interaction, free of inhibition, fear, and shame.

Sexual empowerment is being comfortable with one's self, and being able to share a private zone with another person in a respectful, playful, and spontaneous manner. It is a life-long process of adjustment and growth, only possible when vaginismus is cured.

I've learned a great deal so far in my search for the goddess within. First, that in order to escape the vicious cycle, I must dwell in truth. This means dragging the monsters out from under the bed. Exposing my fears to the light of day has been very difficult, but worthwhile. I've learned that what makes me sexy has to do with what I think of me, not what others think of me. I've learned to speak up about my desires and to communicate what "works" and what does not, sexually and in general. Therapy enabled me to get "back on track" with regard to my sexual development. In many ways, I feel like an adolescent again, thrilled by a new sense of burgeoning power, both sexually and personally. This empowerment flows into every aspect of my life and has improved my relationships with others in many ways. I now realize that my sexuality is a unique and beautiful part of how I express who I am; the physical manifestations of my love and affection. I feel I've wasted far too much time being critical of it, and frightened by it, instead of embracing and enjoying it. Therapy has been a journey of self-acceptance and discovery. It has been scary and difficult at times because it is not easy to peel away layers of denial; of deeply ingrained perceptions and ideas. It has been a journey of faith, requiring me to abandon the safety of long-held misconceptions and troubled behavior patterns. For me, certain aspects of physical "work" needed to be practiced before I could experience any emotional or psychological gain. Sometimes, this felt like I was strapping on a set of wings and sprinting off the nearest cliff! The point is, I grew in therapy in direct proportion to the willingness I displayed in trusting the process, even when my first reaction was reluctance. The old saying "free the mind and the rest will follow" proved to be the key for my success. I have learned that the woman's most vital sex organ lies between the ears, not between the legs.

In conclusion, empowerment is a gift to those who are willing to face the truth and overcome their limitations. It is the inspiration to spread one's wings and soar as high as possible, taking on challenges and experimenting with new ideas. It is confidence, self-assurance, and trust in the powers from within.

Kim's story summarizes it all:

Without question, conquering vaginismus was the single most empowering event of my life. It was at this point that I finally took control of my body, and most importantly, my life. This symbolized a new beginning for me, one where fear and shame were replaced with strength, freedom, and peace.

Although I didn't know there was a name for my problem until years later, I realized something was terribly wrong during my adolescence. To this day, I still recall the terror I felt when my mom bought me my first box of tampons. Simply the sight and idea of putting something into my vagina frightened me. My mom

267

suggested that I get a mirror so that I'd know where to guide the tampon. After several painful and frustrating attempts, I gave up. I was convinced that my vagina was too small to accommodate penetration. Although I was humiliated about my situation, I didn't confide in anyone about my fears. It was particularly difficult when my friends would talk about tampons and sex. Typically, I'd try to change the subject, but other times I'd pretend that everything was fine. I learned quickly, however, that vaginismus couldn't be swept under the carpet and ignored. As suggested by experts, it is about life, not just sex.

A year after the tampon debacle, I entered into my first serious, long-term relationship. After dating for nearly six months, my boyfriend brought up the topic of sex. Despite being petrified, I eventually attempted to have intercourse with him. I hoped that my vaginal opening had miraculously enlarged and that I'd be "normal." Obviously, nothing had changed. I was absolutely devastated when I was unable to have sex. Even though the physical pain was severe, the emotional consequences were far more excruciating. I truly felt like a freak of nature. Sadly, due to my extreme shame, I continued to keep the vaginismus a secret. I was convinced that I was the only one in the world with this problem. As a result, I became depressed and increasingly anxious.

My feelings of inadequacy and hopelessness intensified as the years went by. The college scene was particularly rough for me. It felt like everyone around me was having sex or at least abstaining by choice. I, on the other hand, had no option. I was completely powerless over the situation. When I began dating Eric, my now-husband, I was constantly thinking about how I could get myself off the hook from having sex. While he was patient and understanding, he naturally wanted to have intercourse. I did muster up the courage to try one night, but I knew in my heart that it wasn't going to be successful. Sure enough, after nearly an hour of painful and frustrating attempts, I began crying and told Eric that I wasn't ready and needed to wait until we were married. I desperately wanted to confide in him about my fears, but I was afraid he'd think I was crazy and leave me. Although we refrained from attempting intercourse again for years, feelings of powerlessness began to dominate my life. There wasn't a day that went by that I didn't think about vaginismus. Simple trips to the drugstore became torturous. It was demoralizing, as a young adult, having to buy maxi pads instead of tampons. Similarly, seeing the birth control and internal vaginal products triggered both panic and sadness in me. They were constant reminders of my secret.

Perhaps the biggest crisis occurred during my junior year of college, when I developed a yeast infection. Because of my inability to use internal, over the counter medications, it became increasingly severe. Although I attempted to treat it externally with creams, it continued to worsen to the point where it became painful even to walk. With no other option, I made an appointment to go to the gynecologist, my greatest fear in life. The days leading up to the appointment were agonizing. I was in a constant state of extreme anxiety and panic. My mother, unaware of the depth of my problem, kept saying, "Don't worry, it's no big deal . . . all women go to the gynecologist."

The actual day of the appointment was traumatic. I was shaking and sweating throughout the entire appointment. Not surprisingly, the physician was unable to examine me because I was so tense. Clearly frustrated, she told me that I could become sterile if I didn't treat the infection. She instructed me to go home and drink wine to relax myself. Obviously, this wasn't a viable solution. As a result, a hymenectomy was recommended as a means to "open me up." Desperate, I jumped at this opportunity, hoping it would be a quick fix. Sadly, like other misguided attempts to treat vaginismus, the surgery was unsuccessful. Apart from curing the yeast infection (the doctor used an internal medication while I was under anesthesia), it did not obliterate my fears of penetration. Following this procedure, I waited several years before seeking help again. My self-esteem was suffering tremendously and the profound sense of hopelessness invaded my spirit.

Eric and I got married. While it was a beautiful wedding, the vaginismus definitely cast a cloud over the occasion. It was hard to reconcile the fact that I could not have intercourse with my husband on our wedding night. Although we were intimate in other ways, I felt enormous guilt over my inability to be a "normal" wife. Even though Eric did not understand what was going on, he clearly knew that my problem was there to stay.

Several months after our wedding, I began therapy. It took me a while to confide in my therapist that I was unable to have sex, or any type of vaginal penetration for that matter. While it was incredibly freeing to reveal my secret to someone, the psychotherapy did little to remedy the problem. In fact, I came away believing that I had been sexually abused as a child. Once again, I was left feeling hopeless and powerless.

Several years later, during my graduate studies in social work, I was taking a human sexuality course. It was here where I learned that my problem had an actual name and that I wasn't the only one suffering with it. I immediately began researching the disorder and learned that sex therapy was the preferred treatment approach. With a guarded sense of hope and optimism, I located a sexuality program at a prestigious psychiatric hospital and embarked on therapy once again.

Following several months of therapy, I became increasingly discouraged. The treatment approach focused on relaxation exercises, visual imagery, and homework activities. Essentially, these assignments involved inserting dilators into myself while using the relaxation techniques practiced during therapy. Needless to say, I failed during every attempt. Despite how hard I tried to relax, I was unable to insert even the smallest one. Following each trial, I ended up in tears, feeling completely defeated. Knowing this was clearly not the right approach for me, I discontinued therapy shortly thereafter.

Undeniably, a great toll had been taken on our marriage. I often wondered if Eric regretted marrying me. It seemed that all possible avenues had been pursued and that I had no chance of conquering the vaginismus. I was distraught thinking we would never be able to have biological children, a dream of ours. Similarly, I became paralyzed with insecurity, fearing *that Eric would ultimately leave me, despite his repeated reassurances. During these darkest moments, I became so depressed that I even considered taking my own life. I had reached a point where I lost all sense of myself.*

A few more years passed. I was surfing the Internet and came across the Women's Therapy Center. As I began reading testimonial after testimonial of actual women who had been SUCCESSFULLY treated there, I became flooded with emotion. I was both skeptical and ecstatic at the same time.

Within two months, I was at the center for a two-week rigorous treatment regimen. Although I was scared to death of failing, I knew this might be my one true shot at coming out a winner. By this point, I had confided in my mother and a friend about my situation. Fortunately, they, along with Eric, backed me all the way. The therapy process was an intense, powerful, life-altering experience. While I worked harder than I ever had before, I also experienced joy and growth beyond compare. At the conclusion of treatment, I could use tampons and applicators, undergo a simulated gynecologic exam, and, most importantly, have intercourse with my husband. To my amazement, I was able to do all of these things without any pain or fear!

My experience was nothing short of a dream come true. Conquering vaginismus has changed my life profoundly. I gained so much more than simply the ability to have vaginal penetration. My spirit has been lifted, and I'm now able to truly embrace the world around me. Most important, I have been empowered, and this is perhaps the greatest gift one could ever receive.

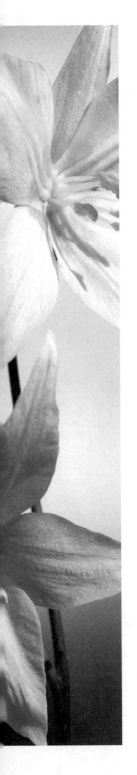

CHAPTER SEVENTEEN

Epilog

*W*e have arrived at our final destination, having brought vaginismus out of its cave of secrecy and into the open.

It is our hope that this book provided you with needed explanations, reassurance, guidance and inspiration to grow, to expand, to search, to believe, and to hope.

Vaginismus needs your voice—the voice of the woman who suffers; the voice of the partner who cares; the voice of the professional who wishes to help but does not know how; the voices of family members and of members of the clergy; the voice of anyone else who feels the anguish. We should all team up . . . merge our voices, our strength, and our knowledge and embark on a new journey, that of curing vaginismus!

🌸🌸🌸

Eve, a nineteen-year-old single student wrote chapter two, "The Girl Without a Hole," in which she mentioned attending a costume party dressed as the Greek goddess Artemis, the goddess of the moon, the hunt, and virginity.

A few months following the conclusion of her own treatment process, Eve wished to speak in the name of all women who suffer from the condition. She wrote the following poem as her tribute to freedom from vaginismus:

Artemis and Vaginismus*
by Eve F.
April 2000

Oh Mother Leto, Father Zeus,
At last you'll know my truth.
It was no joke.
It was not my choice.
I never did ask to be a hunted prey,
Impossible to love,
Immune to rape,
As legend declares so confidently
That even your immortal memories
Were deceived into believing.
My precious moonflower was not afraid to bloom.
It was unconscious,
It was stuck.

And so was I,
Sentenced to childhood forever,
Beneath my restless moonlight.
I pleaded for help,
But you could not conceive of my pain
As easily as you conceived me
In an accidental moment of perilous passion.
As your unwarranted progeny,
I was punished by Queen Hera
With an everlasting, disordered virginity.
But I broke her spell.
I traveled alone in my chariot
Over obstacles unknown and for hours too exhaustive to recall,
To a chamber of torture and torturous recovery,
Where Aphrodite gently and firmly
Helped conquer my fate.
Now you'll watch in shock
As I pronounce to others,
Struggling in the thick, nocturnal forests,
That they, too, can be free of the moon's chaste confinement.
And although I've escaped from my title of innocence,
My power to guide has become stronger.
I shed fresh moonlight on the alone and misunderstood,
As you never could.
For just as I was not what I seemed,
You are not omniscient gods.

❦ ❦ ❦

*Vaginismus is a curable physical, mental, and emotional disorder in women, in which penetration is painful or impossible. Unfortunately, it is only beginning to gain the much-needed publicity.

Resources and References

The authors' Website, **www.womentc.com**, includes extensive information about female sexual health, as well as their publications, media features, and professional biography. Make sure to revisit the site for updates and new information.

Books about Women's Health:

A New View of a Woman's Body,
by Federation of Feminist Women's Health Center

For Yourself: The Fulfillment of Female Sexuality,
by Lonnie Barbach, Ph.D.

For Women Only:
A Revolutionary Guide to Overcoming
Sexual Dysfunction and Reclaiming Your Sex Life,
by Jennifer Berman, M.D., and Laura Berman, Ph.D.

KISS Guide to Sex,
by Anne Hooper

Our Bodies, Ourselves for the New Century:
A Book by and for Women,
by Boston Women's Health Book Collective

The Clitoral Truth:
The Secret World at Your Fingertips,
by Rebecca Chalker

The Magic of Sex,
by Miriam Stoppard, M.D.

Venus in Blue Jeans:
Why Mothers and Daughters Need to Talk about Sex,
by Nathalie A. Bartle and Susan A. Lieberman

Books about Female Adolescents' Health and Sexuality:

101 Ways to Help Your Daughter Love Her Body,
by Brenda Lane Richardson and Elane Rehr

Changing Bodies, Changing Lives:
A Book for Teens on Sex and Relationships,
by Ruth Bell Alexander

Ophelia Speaks:
Adolescent Girls Write about Their Search for Self,
by Sara Shandler

Sweetie, Here's the Best Reason on the Planet to Say
No to Your Boyfriend Even If You've Already Said Yes,
by Debra J. Plalardy

The Underground Guide to Teenage Sexuality:
An Essential Handbook for Today's Teens and Parents,
by Michael J. Basso

Books about Pregnancy:

Conception, Pregnancy, and Birth,
by Miriam Stoppard, M.D.

Dr. Miriam Stoppard's New Pregnancy and Birth Book,
by Miriam Stoppard, M.D.

What to Expect When You're Expecting (Revised Edition),
by Arlene Eisenberg, Sandee E. Hathaway,
and Heidi E. Murkoff

Books about Sex Therapy:

Illustrated Manual of Sex Therapy,
by Helen Singer Kaplan and David Passalacqua

Principles and Practice of Sex Therapy (3rd ed.),
by Sandra Risa Leiblum

Sexual Dysfunction:
A Guide for Assessment and Treatment,
by John P. Wincze, Michael P. Carey

Treating Sexual Disorders,
edited by Randolph S. Charlton

Women's Health and Sexuality Websites:

www.medscape.com

www.wwwomen.com

www.womenswire.com

www.achoo.com/main.asp

www.gyn101.com

www.mentalhelp.net

www.womens-health.com

www.myvag.net/mound.shtml

www.self.com

Birth Control Websites

www.plannedparenthood.com

Men's Sexuality Websites

www.the-penis.com

www.menshealth.com

Sexually Transmitted Diseases Websites

www.bestd.org/stds.htm

Sex Therapy Organization Websites

www.sexologist.org

www.aasect.org

Medical References

Coplan JD, Lydiard RB. Brain circuits in panic disorder. Biol Psychiatry 1998 Dec 15;44(12):1264-1276.

Dixon J and Goling J. Histomorphology of Pelvic Floor Muscle. In Schussler B, Laycock J, Norton P, Stanton S (eds): Pelvic Floor Re-education. Springer-Verlag, 1994 pp30-31.

Herzer CM. Toxic shock syndrome: broadening the differential diagnosis. J Am Board Fam Pract 2001 Mar-Apr;14(2):131-136.

LeDoux JE. Emotion circuits in the brain. Annu Rev Neurosci 2000;23(4):155-184.

McKay M. Vulvodynia. In Steege JF, Metzger DA, Levy BS (eds): Chronic Pelvic Pain. Philadelphia, WB Saunders, 1998, pp188-196.

Nesse RM. Proximate and evolutionary studies of anxiety, stress and depression: synergy at the interface. Neuroscience and Biobehavioral Review 1999 (23):895-903.

Nesse RM., Young EA. The evolutionary origins and functions of the stress response. 1999 February. Randolph M Nesse, the University of Michigan, 5057 ISR, 426 Thompson Street, Ann Arbor, MI 48106-1248

Omar HA, Aggarwal S, Perkins KC. Tampon use in young women. J Pediatr Adolesc Gynecol 1998 Aug;11(3):143-146.

Roger, RM Jr: Basic Pelvic Neuroanatomy. In Steege JF, Metzger DA, Levy BS (eds): Chronic Pelvic Pain. Philadelphia, WB Saunders, 1998, pp31-68.

Schultz WW, van Andel P, Sabelis I, Mooyaart E. Magnetic resonance imaging of male and female genitals during coitus and female sexual arousal. BMJ 1999 December; 319:1596-1600.

van der Velde J, Laan E, Everaerd W. Vaginismus, a component of a general defense reaction. An investigation of pelvic floor muscle activity during exposure to emotion-inducing film excerpts in women with and without vaginismus. Int Urogynecol J 2001;12:328-331.

Glossary

Adrenal gland—A triangular-shaped gland that is attached to the top of each kidney. It secretes different substances that regulate all the systems in the body.

Anus—The external opening at the end of the digestive system (rectum) through which the stool passes.

Artificial insemination—The introduction of semen into the uterus or the ovary by means other than intercourse.

Autonomic Nervous System—The component of the Central Nervous System that is not subject to voluntary control as it regulates individual organ function and homeostasis (body temperature, pH of blood, etc.).

Bladder—A distensible muscular sac that is situated in the pelvis in front of the rectum, and serves as a temporary retention of urine until it is being discharged by urination.

Cervix—The lower end of the uterus, which also serves as its opening.

Chemotherapy—The use of chemical agents (medications) in the treatment of certain diseases.

Clitoris—A small, erectile organ at the front of the vulva. It is the site of female sexual stimulation and orgasm, just like the male's penis.

Clitoral glans—The tip of the clitoris: a pea-shaped structure containing a high concentration of blood vessels and nerves, which make it extremely sensitive to sexual stimulation. Developmentally, it is similar to the head of the male's penis.

Clitoral hood—A fold of skin that covers the clitoral glans, similar to the foreskin on the male's penis.

Condom—A sheath commonly of rubber, worn either over the penis or inserted into the vagina to prevent conception (pregnancy) and/or the spreading of sexually transmitted diseases.

Dilator—An instrument for expanding or stretching a tube-like structure.

Dyspareunia—Difficult or painful sexual intercourse.

Fight-or-flight response—Changes in the body in response to danger, caused by activation of the Sympathetic Nervous System, which prepares the body to fight or to flee (run away, fast!).

Foreplay—Erotic stimulation preceding intercourse or outer-course.

General anesthesia—Being under the influence of such drugs as those that block sensations in the body by producing complete unconsciousness, as used during surgery.

Genitals—The organs of the reproductive and sexual stimulation system. In females, they include the clitoris, vulva, vagina, urethra, uterus, fallopian tubes, and ovaries. In males, they include the penis, testes, the urethra, the prostate gland, and their internal ducts.

Heterosexual—Sexual attraction toward the opposite sex.

Homosexual—Sexual attraction toward the same sex.

Hormones—Substances that are secreted by certain organs and glands in the body, and which then circulate through the bloodstream to distant parts for stimulating specific activities or production of other hormones.

Hymen—A thin membrane that partially or wholly closes the opening of the vagina. The hymen is located a short way into the vagina and varies in size, shape, and thickness from woman to woman.

Hysterectomy—A surgical procedure to remove the uterus. A radical hysterectomy refers to a more extensive surgery that also includes removing the ovaries, fallopian tubes, cervix, and vaginal tissue next to the cervix.

Involuntary muscles—Muscles that are responsible for reflex functions (automatic contractions) and are not under the person's conscious control.

Labia Majora—The outer fatty folds of the vulva.

Labia Minora—The inner, highly vascular and sensitive folds of the vulva.

Masturbation—Sexual stimulation of one's own body, primarily the genitals, to produce pleasure and orgasm. Female masturbation does not necessarily include any vaginal insertion.

Menopause—The time in a woman's life that begins one year after her last menstrual period, usually occurring between ages forty-five and fifty-five.

Orgasm—A series of muscle contractions of the pelvic diaphragm that signal the climax of sexual excitation.

Outercourse—Sexual activities that do not involve vaginal penetration.

PAP smear—Named after Dr. George N. Papanicolaou, who invented this method of detecting uterine cancer by taking tissue samples from the cervix and the surrounding vaginal canal. This test is also called Papanicolaou test, Papanicolaou smear, or Pap test.

Pelvic diaphragm—The "sling-like" muscles of the pelvic floor that stretch from front to back and from side to side, separating the pelvic organs from the outer skin and assisting bowel and bladder control, producing orgasms, and resisting unwanted penetration.

Penis—The male's organ of urination, reproduction, sexual pleasure and orgasm.

Pubic bone—The lower portion of the pelvic bone, right above the genitals.

Rectum—The lower portion of the digestive system, ending in the anus.

Speculum—An instrument used for insertion into a body opening (i.e., vagina or nasal passages) to hold it open for looking in, or for applying medication or surgical instruments. A speculum may be made of metal or plastic, and come in different sizes.

Sperm—The male's impregnating cell: a microscopic structure that is shaped like a tadpole, swims in seminal fluid, and is introduced into the woman's fallopian tubes during ejaculation in the hope of uniting with an egg and culminating in pregnancy.

Stirrups—The footrests of the examining table at the gynecologist's office, used during a pelvic exam.

Urethra—The tube that carries the urine from the bladder to the outside of the body. In the male it also serves as the genital tract.

Urinary tract infection (UTI)—An infection of the bladder, typically caused by different bacteria, and with symptoms of burning, frequent urination, pain, pressure, stress, etc.

Uterus—The expandable, muscular sac in a woman's pelvis where pregnancy takes place. The uterus has an inner lining (endometrium), which undergoes changes every month: It thickens in the first half of the menstrual cycle in preparation for pregnancy, then sloughs off the excess membrane in what becomes the menstrual flow if pregnancy has not commenced.

Vagina—The elastic, tube-shaped structure that connects the vulva with the uterus. The vagina is a "potential space": The walls touch each other just like a sock; once penetration is attempted, the walls separate and can accommodate a variety of shapes and sizes, be they a penis, a finger, a tampon, a speculum, a surgical instrument, etc.

Vaginismus—An involuntary, instantaneous tightening of the pelvic floor diaphragm, making vaginal penetration difficult or impossible.

Vulva—The external parts of the female genital organs, including the labia majora, labia minora, clitoris, urethral opening, and vaginal opening.

About the Authors

*D*ITZA KATZ, PT, PH.D., is the founder of WOMEN'S THERAPY CENTER, a practice limited to treating women's sexual disorders, urogynecologic dysfunctions, abuse, and trauma. She holds an undergraduate degree in Physical Therapy, a Master's degree in Pastoral Psychology and Counseling, a doctorate in Clinical Sexology, and clinical training in manual therapy and urogynecology. Dr. Katz, assistant professor of clinical sexology at Maimonides University and a Diplomate with the American Board of Sexology, is the only physical therapist in the U.S. who is a clinical sexologist.

*R*OSS LYNN TABISEL, CSW, PH.D., is Co-Director of the WOMEN'S THERAPY CENTER, a Diplomate with the American Board of Sexology, and an assistant professor of clinical sexology at Maimonides University. She holds a Master's degree in Social Work from Adelphi University, a Post-Graduate Certificate in Psychotherapy and Psychoanalysis from the Institute for the Study of Psychotherapy in New York, a doctorate in Clinical Sexology, and Certificate Training in the area of Sexual Abuse. Dr. Tabisel is the first Social Worker to be accepted as a member of the American Urogynecologic Society and of the American College of Obstetrics and Gynecology on the merit of her expertise.

Together, **Dr. Katz** and **Dr. Tabisel** pioneered the ***DiRoss Treatment Approach,*** a successful intervention for vaginismus, for which they have become known worldwide. Because of their expertise, they have been invited lecturers, nationally and internationally, educating healthcare professionals about their unique team approach to female sexual dysfunctions. Media appearances include NBC's *Nightly News*, *Glamour*, *Lifetime Online*, *Newsday*, and their videotape documentary about vaginismus. Publications include articles in medical books, professional journals, and online professional publications. Speaking engagements include professional presentations worldwide, as well as extensive community outreach, educating women of all ages about their sexual health.

To inquire about training seminars,

to arrange speaking engagements,

or to relay your comments/feedback,

please contact the authors at

www.womentc.com